Article 26

The Right to Benefit from Social Security

A Commentary on the United Nations Convention
on the Rights of the Child

Editors

André Alen, Johan Vande Lanotte, Eugeen Verhellen,
Fiona Ang, Eva Berghmans and Mieke Verheyde

Article 26

The Right to Benefit from Social Security

By

Wouter Vandenhole

UNICEF Chair in Children's Rights at the University of Antwerp (Belgium)
Senior researcher at the Center for Transboundary Legal Development,
Tilburg University (the Netherlands)

MARTINUS
NIJHOFF
PUBLISHERS

LEIDEN • BOSTON
2007

This book is printed on acid-free paper.

A Cataloging-in-Publication record for this book is available from the Library of Congress.

Cite as: W. Vandenhole, "Article 26: The Right to Benefit from Social Security", in: A. Alen, J. Vande Lanotte, E. Verhellen, F. Ang, E. Berghmans and M. Verheyde (Eds.) *A Commentary on the United Nations Convention on the Rights of the Child* (Martinus Nijhoff Publishers, Leiden, 2007).

ISSN 1574-8626
ISBN 978-90-04-14879-6

© 2007 by Koninklijke Brill NV, Leiden, The Netherlands.
Koninklijke Brill NV incorporates the imprints Brill, Hotei Publishers, IDC Publishers, Martinus Nijhoff Publishers and VSP.

Cover image by Nadia, 1$^1/_2$ years old

http://www.brill.nl

PRINTED IN THE NETHERLANDS

CONTENTS

LIST OF ABBREVIATIONS

CEACR	ILO Committee of Experts on the Application of Conventions and Recommendations
CEDAW	Convention on the Elimination of All Forms of Discrimination against Women
CERD	Convention on the Elimination of All Forms of Racial Discrimination
CESCR	International Covenant on Economic, Social and Cultural Rights
CRC	Convention on the Rights of the Child
ECHR	European Convention on Human Rights
ECSR	European Committee of Social Rights
ECtHR	European Court of Human Rights
ESC	European Social Charter
IACtHR	Inter-American Court of Human Rights
ICRMW	International Convention on the Protection of the Rights of All Migrant Workers and Members of Their Families
ILO	International Labour Organisation
RESC	Revised European Social Charter
UDHR	Universal Declaration of Human Rights
UNICEF	United Nations Children's Fund

AUTHOR BIOGRAPHY

Wouter Vandenhole is a Belgian scholar who holds the UNICEF Chair in Children's Rights at the University of Antwerp (Belgium). He is also a senior researcher at the Center for Transboundary Legal Development, Tilburg University (the Netherlands). He graduated in law at the University of Leuven (Belgium), obtained an LL.M. in Law in Development from the University of Warwick (United Kingdom) and holds a PhD from the University of Leuven. He has previously held positions at the University of Leuven and at the European Master's Degree Programme in Human Rights and Democratisation (Venice, Italy). His research interests include human rights, in particular economic, social and cultural rights, and the relationship between human rights law and development. He is the author of *Non-Discrimination and Equality in the View of the UN Human Rights Treaty Bodies* (Antwerp, Intersentia, 2005) and *The Procedures Before the UN Human Rights Treaty Bodies: Divergence or Convergence?* (Antwerp, Intersentia, 2004), and has co-edited *Protocol No. 14 and the Reform of the European Court of Human Rights* (Antwerp, Intersentia, 2005).

TEXT OF ARTICLE 26

ARTICLE 26

1. States Parties shall recognize for every child the right to benefit from social security, including social insurance, and shall take the necessary measures to achieve the full realization of this right in accordance with their national law.

2. The benefits should, where appropriate, be granted, taking into account the resources and the circumstances of the child and persons having responsibility for the maintenance of the child, as well as any other consideration relevant to an application for benefits made by or on behalf of the child.

ARTICLE 26

1. Les Etats parties reconnaissent à tout enfant le droit de bénéficier de la sécurité sociale, y compris les assurances sociales, et prennent les mesures nécessaires pour assurer la pleine réalisation de ce droit en conformité avec leur législation nationale.

2. Les prestations doivent, lorsqu'il y a lieu, être accordées compte tenu des ressources et de la situation de l'enfant et des personnes responsables de son entretien, ainsi que de toute autre considération applicable à la demande de prestation faite par l'enfant ou en son nom.

CHAPTER ONE

INTRODUCTION*

1. The right to (benefit from) social security is under pressure. For some at least, the right has become outdated, as has the social welfare state, with which it is often automatically associated. The rise of neo-liberal doctrine in social policy-making has led to cutting back on public expenditure, and to privatisation and marketisation of the State,[1] leading to the demise of the social welfare state as traditionally understood. However, as the UN Committee on Economic, Social and Cultural Rights (CESCR Committee) pointed out as far back as 1990, 'in terms of political and economic systems the [CESCR] is neutral.' The CRC in general, and the right to benefit from social security – as guaranteed by Article 26 of the CRC – in particular, are beyond ideology too. The right to benefit from social security is also today an important right, both in itself and for the realisation of other rights in the CRC (*Cf. infra* No. 17–19).

2. Delineation of the right to benefit from social security from the right to an adequate standard of living, as guaranteed in Article 27 of the CRC, is sometimes difficult and may be slightly artificial. Moreover, the CRC Committee often seems to ignore the distinction, and addresses both rights under one and the same heading in its concluding observations. Nonetheless, a distinction between the two rights can and should be made. The right to benefit from social security and the right to an adequate standard of living do not coincide, although social security can be one of the avenues for guaranteeing the right to an adequate standard of living. Article 26 of the CRC should not be read in disconnection from similar provisions in other human rights treaties, in which social security has a specific and technical meaning (*inter alia* implying the nine traditional branches of social security), based

---

* December 2006.

[1] See, *e.g.*, H. Stocke, 'What Is Left of State Responsibility? Turning State Obligations into State Responsibility in the Field of Economic, Social and Cultural Rights', in: M. Scheinin and M. Suksi (eds.), *Human Rights in Development Yearbook 2002: Empowerment, Participation, Accountability and Non-Discrimimation: Operationalising a Human Rights-Based Approach to Development* (Leiden, Martinus Nijhoff, 2005), pp. 41–50 in particular.

on the ILO conventions in the field of social security (*Cf. infra* Nos. 10 and following). By adhering to the specific and technical meaning of the right, the CRC Committee might sometimes be able to offer children enhanced protection in practice. The interpretation of Article 26 of the CRC should therefore be guided by the ILO conventions and the conceptual analysis of the right to social security by the CESCR Committee and the European Committee of Social Rights (ECSR). Extensive reference will therefore be made to their jurisprudence.

3. In the next chapter, related international human rights and ILO provisions will be briefly presented. In chapter three, the scope of Article 26 of the CRC will be explored, both in light of its subject and its object, and of the obligations for States. The analysis of the latter will be mainly based on the organizing principles of Article 9 of the CESCR and Article 12 of the (Revised) European Social Charter ((R)ESC). Article 12 of the (R)ESC is structured along four paragraphs, in which four guarantees are offered: the existence or maintenance of a system of social security; a minimum standard; the progressive improvement of the system; and non-discrimination. The CESCR Committee has analysed the right to social security in light of its interdependent elements of availability, accessibility and quality.

CHAPTER TWO

COMPARISON WITH RELATED INTERNATIONAL
HUMAN RIGHTS PROVISIONS

4. The right to social security is guaranteed in a large number of universal and regional human rights treaties. In what follows, the relevant provisions in the Universal Declaration of Human Rights (UDHR), the Convention on the Elimination of All Forms of Racial Discrimination (CERD), the Convention on the Elimination of All Forms of Discrimination against Women (CEDAW), the International Covenant on Economic, Social and Cultural Rights (CESCR) and the International Convention on the Protection of the Rights of All Migrant Workers and Members of Their Families (ICRMW) will be introduced. Attention will also be paid to the ILO Social Security (Minimum Standards) Convention No. 102, amongst others, which is explicitly or implicitly a point of reference for many of the social security provisions in human rights treaties. Finally, the right to social security as guaranteed within the regional systems for human rights protection will be scrutinized.

1. *Universal Human Rights Provisions*

1.1. *Human Rights Declarations and Treaties*

5. Article 25(1) of the UDHR (1948) reads:

> Everyone has the right to a standard of living adequate for the health and well-being of himself and his family, including food, clothing, housing and medical care and necessary social services, and the right to social security in the event of unemployment, sickness, disability, widowhood, old age or other lack of livelihood in circumstances beyond his control.

Article 25(1) of the UDHR (1948) refers to both social welfare (an adequate standard of living) and social security in one single paragraph. With regard to social security, it enumerates particular risks to be covered, such as unemployment, illness, disability, widowhood and old age. It thus contains a more specific provision on social security than the CRC.

6. CERD (1965) contains a general reference to the right to social security in the specific context of the prohibition of racial discrimination. In Article 5

of the CERD, States Parties undertake to eliminate racial discrimination and to guarantee equality before the law *inter alia* in the enjoyment of the right to social security:

> In compliance with the fundamental obligations laid down in Article 2 of this Convention, States Parties undertake to prohibit and to eliminate racial discrimination in all its forms and to guarantee the right of everyone, without distinction as to race, colour, or national or ethnic origin, to equality before the law, notably in the enjoyment of the following rights:
> [...]
> (e) Economic, social and cultural rights, in particular:
> [...]
> (iv) The right to public health, medical care, social security and social services;

7. Much in line with Article 26 of the CRC, a very general and extremely short provision on the right to social security can be found in Article 9 of the CESCR (1966):

> The States Parties to the present Covenant recognize the right of everyone to social security, including social insurance.

The intention of the drafters was to include a short and general clause on the right to social security in the Covenant, thereby leaving it to the specialised agencies of the UN, and in particular the ILO, to sort out the details.[2]

Article 10(2) of the CESCR offers special protection to mothers before and after childbirth, during which period 'working mothers should be accorded paid leave or leave with adequate social security benefits.'

8. Article 11(1) of the CEDAW (1979) is more specific than Article 26 of the CRC, in that it contains references to a number of specific risks (as the UDHR does), such as retirement, unemployment, sickness, invalidity and old age. However, in line with the overall purpose of the treaty, only the *equal right* to social security of women is guaranteed:

> 1. States Parties shall take all appropriate measures to eliminate discrimination against women in the field of employment in order to ensure, on a basis of equality of men and women, the same rights, in particular:
> [...]
> (e) The right to social security, particularly in cases of retirement, unemployment, sickness, invalidity and old age and other incapacity to work, as well as the right to paid leave.

---

[2] Commission on Human Rights, *Summary Record of the Two Hundred and Twentieth Meeting* (UN Doc. E/CN.4/SR.220), p. 13.

Article 14(2) of the CEDAW deals with discrimination against women in rural areas in particular. It reads:

> States Parties shall take all appropriate measures to eliminate discrimination against women in rural areas in order to ensure, on a basis of equality of men and women, that they participate in and benefit from rural development and, in particular, shall ensure to such women the right:
> [...]
> (c) To benefit directly from social security programmes.

9. Provisions on the right to social security in the ICRMW (1990) again mainly deal with equality of treatment. Article 27 of the ICRMW reads:

> 1. With respect to social security, migrant workers and members of their families shall enjoy in the State of employment the same treatment granted to nationals in so far as they fulfil the requirements provided for by the applicable legislation of that State and the applicable bilateral and multilateral treaties. The competent authorities of the State of origin and the State of employment can at any time establish the necessary arrangements to determine the modalities of application of this norm.
> 2. Where the applicable legislation does not allow migrant workers and members of their families a benefit, the States concerned shall examine the possibility of reimbursing interested persons the amount of contributions made by them with respect to that benefit on the basis of the treatment granted to nationals who are in similar circumstances.

Article 61(3) of the ICRMW concerning project-tied workers reads:

> Subject to bilateral or multilateral agreements in force for them, the States Parties concerned shall endeavour to enable project-tied workers to remain adequately protected by the social security systems of their States of origin or habitual residence during their engagement in the project. States Parties concerned shall take appropriate measures with the aim of avoiding any denial of rights or duplication of payments in this respect.

1.2. ILO Conventions

10. The International Labour Organisation (ILO) is the main locus of standard-setting and implementation in the field of social security.[3] ILO conventions on social security are a central source of interpretation for

---

[3] M. Scheinin, 'The Right to Social Security', in: A. Eide, C. Krause and A. Rosas (eds.), *Economic, Social and Cultural Rights* (Dordrecht/Boston/London, Martinus Nijhoff Publishers, 2001), pp. 214–215.

human rights provisions on social security.[4] Some basic ILO conventions on social security are therefore briefly discussed here, although they are strictly speaking not human rights treaties.

11. In 1952, ILO Social Security (Minimum Standards) Convention No. 102 was adopted. As of 1 December 2006, 42 States had ratified this Convention. Convention No. 102 covers the following nine social risks, which were considered to constitute the main branches of any social security system: health care, sickness benefit, unemployment benefit, old-age benefit, employment injury benefit, family benefit, maternity benefit, invalidity benefit and survivor's benefit. Each State Party is to comply with at least three of the benefits covered, in which at least one of the following five hard core branches is to be included: unemployment benefit, old-age benefit, employment injury benefit, invalidity benefit or survivor's benefit (Article 2).

The respective provisions contain *minimum levels and duration* of benefits, as well as minimum coverage of a certain percentage of certain *categories* or classes. These categories are determined in three different ways, according to the preference of the State: by reference to employees, the economically active population or the resident population. A third basic concept in ILO Convention No. 102 is that of *periodic payments* of social security.[5]

The core characteristics of a social security system can be found in the Articles 71 and 72: the costs to be born by employees should not be excessive; responsibility for the economic health of the system is to be taken by a public authority; participation of the beneficiaries in the administration of the system is to be provided for; and a right to appeal is to be available in case of refusal of a benefit, as well as a right of complaint about the quantity or quality of benefits.[6]

Other, subsequent ILO Conventions that deal with specific branches of social security and contain more specific rules are amongst others, the Employment Injury Benefits Convention No. 121 (1964), the Invalidity, Old-Age and Survivors' Benefits Convention No. 128 (1967), the Medical Care and Sickness Benefits Convention No. 130 (1969) and Employment Promotion and Protection against Unemployment Convention No. 168 (1988).

---

[4] L. Lamarche, 'The Right to Social Security in the International Covenant on Economic, Social and Cultural Rights', in: A. Chapman and S. Russell (eds.), *Core Obligations: Building a Framework for Economic, Social and Cultural Rights* (Antwerp/Oxford/New York, Intersentia, 2002), p. 95.
[5] *Ibid.*, p. 91.
[6] *Ibid.*, p. 94.

Compliance is monitored by the ILO Committee of Experts on the Application of Conventions and Recommendations (CEACR).

2. Regional Treaties

2.1. Europe

12. Article 12 of the (Revised) European Social Charter (1996) guarantees the right to social security. It reads:

With a view to ensuring the effective exercise of the right to social security, the Parties undertake:

1. to establish or maintain a system of social security;
2. to maintain the social security system at a satisfactory level at least equal to that necessary for the ratification of the European Code of Social Security;
3. to endeavour to raise progressively the system of social security to a higher level;
4. to take steps, by the conclusion of appropriate bilateral and multilateral agreements or by other means, and subject to the conditions laid down in such agreements, in order to ensure:
   a. equal treatment with their own nationals of the nationals of other Parties in respect of social security rights, including the retention of benefits arising out of social security legislation, whatever movements the persons protected may undertake between the territories of the Parties;
   b. the granting, maintenance and resumption of social security rights by such means as the accumulation of insurance or employment periods completed under the legislation of each of the Parties.

Article 12 of the (R)ESC contains four principles: first of all, a social security system is to be established or maintained. Secondly, a minimum level is defined for that social security system. Thirdly, the principle of progressive improvement of the system is provided for. Finally, in the fourth paragraph, measures are encouraged to ensure equality of treatment for the nationals of other contracting States, as well as the granting, maintenance and resumption of social security rights.[7]

The text of Article 12 is the same in the 1961 European Social Charter and the 1996 Revised European Social Charter, except for paragraph 2, in which the minimum level is defined. Whereas in the 1961 Charter reference is made to ILO Convention No. 102, the 1996 text refers to the European Code

---

[7] ECSR, *Conclusions* I, 1969–70, p. 62.

of Social Security, a Council of Europe instrument. Both treaties are very similar in the branches they cover, but the minimum requirements of acceptance for ratification are twice as high for the Code (*i.e.* six compared to three as required for the ILO Convention). The ratification of the European Code thus requires a higher standard of social security than is required for the ratification of ILO Convention No. 102.[8] Moreover, in the European Code of Social Security *all* workers are covered, whereas under ILO Convention No. 102 seamen and sea fishermen are excluded.[9] The European Code of Social Security covers sickness and maternity, invalidity, old-age and survivor's benefits, occupational injuries and disease benefits, death grants, unemployment and family benefits. It was signed in 1964. As of 1 December 2006, it had been ratified by 20 mainly Western European states. A Protocol was adopted in 1964, allowing States to achieve a higher level of social security than that provided for in the provisions of the Code. The Revised European Code of Social Security (1990) has not yet entered into force, although only two ratifications are required.

Article 13 of the (R)ESC deals with the right to social assistance, which falls outside the scope of the ILO concept of social security.[10] Article 14 of the (R)ESC guarantees the right to benefit from social welfare services. Articles 16 and 17 deal with specific forms of social security and/or social welfare, such as family benefits and services for mothers and children.

Both Articles 12 and 13 belong to the 'hard-core' provisions of the (R)ESC.[11] The (R)ESC applies an '*à-la-carte*' system, *i.e.* States Parties choose which provisions they consider themselves bound by. Certain rules are to be observed nevertheless. Under the ESC, out of seven hard-core articles, to which the article on the right to social security belongs, States Parties are to accept at least five. In addition, they have to select a number of articles or numbered paragraphs, so that they are at least bound by ten articles or 45 numbered paragraphs.[12] Under the RESC, States are to consider themselves bound by at least six of the nine hard-core provisions (among which

---

[8] *Explanatory Report to the Revised European Social Charter*, paras. 57–58.
[9] L. Samuel, *Fundamental Social Rights. Case Law of the European Social Charter* (Strasbourg, Council of Europe Publishing, 2002), p. 287.
[10] M. Scheinin, *l.c.* (note 3), p. 216.
[11] ECSR, 'General consideration on certain areas covered by the Charter: social protection, General Introduction', *Conclusions* XIII–4, p. 35.
[12] Article 20 of the ESC.

again Article 12 on the right to social security), and to 16 articles or 63 numbered paragraphs in total.[13]

States are only obliged to provide family benefits if they have accepted Article 16 of the (R)ESC. Family allowances fall within the scope of Article 16 because it specifically includes family benefits as a means of promoting the welfare of the family. The existence of a family benefits scheme is a *sufficient* but not *necessary* condition for compliance with Article 12, but it is a necessary condition for fulfilling Article 16. A State can comply with Article 12 without providing family benefits, for family benefits constitute only one of the nine branches of social security, and compliance with Article 12 does not require coverage of all nine branches. However, if a State has accepted Article 16, it has accepted a more specific obligation than that of Article 12, *i.e.* an obligation to protect the family through various measures, including the provision of family benefits.[14]

13. Article 34 of the Charter of Fundamental Rights of the European Union, a declaration adopted in 2000, deals with social security and social assistance.[15] The entitlement to social security benefits and social services is recognized with regard to five explicitly mentioned risks: maternity, illness, industrial accidents, dependency or old age, and unemployment. No explicit mention is made of child benefits, although children may be assumed to be covered by the concept of dependency. It reads:

> 1. The Union recognises and respects the entitlement to social security benefits and social services providing protection in cases such as maternity, illness, industrial accidents, dependency or old age, and in the case of loss of employment, in accordance with the rules laid down by Union law and national laws and practices.
> 2. Everyone residing and moving legally within the European Union is entitled to social security benefits and social advantages in accordance with Union law and national laws and practices.
> 3. In order to combat social exclusion and poverty, the Union recognises and respects the right to social and housing assistance so as to ensure a decent existence for all those who lack sufficient resources, in accordance with the rules laid down by Union law and national laws and practices.

The Charter has been integrated in part II of the Treaty Establishing a Constitution for Europe. The provisions on the entitlement to social security

---

[13] Article A, Part III of the RESC.
[14] ECSR, *Conclusions* XI–1: Denmark.
[15] *Official Journal C 36*, 18 December 2000, pp. 1–22.

benefits can be found in Article II–94. The treaty has not yet entered into force.

2.2. *The Americas*

14. In the Inter-American System, Article 16 of the American Declaration of the Rights and Duties of Men guarantees the right to social security in a limited number of specified areas:

> Every person has the right to social security which will protect him from the consequences of unemployment, old age, and any disabilities arising from causes beyond his control that make it physically or mentally impossible for him to earn a living.

Article 9 of the 1988 Additional Protocol to the American Convention on Human Rights in the Area of Economic, Social and Cultural Rights (the so-called 'Protocol of San Salvador') holds specific provisions on old age and disability benefits for everyone, as well as on social security benefits for employees in the field of health care, work-related injuries or diseases, and maternity:

> 1. Everyone shall have the right to social security protecting him from the consequences of old age and of disability which prevents him, physically or mentally, from securing the means for a dignified and decent existence. In the event of the death of a beneficiary, social security benefits shall be applied to his dependents.
> 2. In the case of persons who are employed, the right to social security shall cover at least medical care and an allowance or retirement benefit in the case of work accidents or occupational disease and, in the case of women, paid maternity leave before and after childbirth.

No individual complaints on violations of the right to social security are allowed.[16]

2.3. *Africa*

15. In the African regional system of human rights protection, the right to social security has not as such been recognized as an autonomous human right, neither in the African Charter on Human and Peoples' Rights (1981) nor in the African Charter on the Rights and Well-Being of Children (1990). An explanation for the omission in the former instrument may be found in

---

[16] See Article 19(6) *a contrario*, in which the possibility of individual complaints is provided for with regard to the right to form and join trade unions, and the right to education.

the different political ideologies that confronted each other at the time of drafting the African Charter on Human and Peoples' Rights.[17] The emphasis on duties of the individual, *e.g.* to maintain one's parents in case of need,[18] may offer another explanation for leaving out the right to social security. It might be argued that in an African worldview, taking care of those in need is not so much a task of the State, but rather of the community and the family.[19]

3. Relation with Other CRC Provisions

16. During the drafting process, the question was asked whether the right to benefit from social security had any added value, for Articles 18 and 27 of the CRC covered already concerns addressed by Article 26 of the CRC.

Article 18(2) of the CRC obligates States to render appropriate assistance to parents and guardians in the performance of their child-rearing responsibilities. In Article 27 of the CRC, States recognize the right of every child to 'a standard of living adequate for the child's physical, mental, spiritual, moral and social development', and commit themselves to 'take appropriate measures to assist parents and others responsible for the child to implement this right and shall in case of need provide material assistance and support programmes, particularly with regard to nutrition, clothing and housing'. The ILO argued in favour of retention of Article 26 of the CRC. It submitted that the Articles 18 and 27 'only dealt with specific aspects and did not expressly mention social security'.[20] In the end, Article 26 of the CRC was retained.

17. The CRC Committee seemingly finds it difficult to draw clear lines between the Articles 26 and 27. Quite often, the Committee has made recommendations with regard to social security while referring explicitly to Article 27

---

[17] F. Ouguergouz, *The African Charter on Human and Peoples' Rights. A Comprehensive Agenda for Human Dignity and Sustainable Development in Africa* (The Hague, Martinus Nijhoff, 2003), p. 42.

[18] Article 29, para. 1 of the African Charter on Human and Peoples' Rights.

[19] *Cf. infra* No. 18 for the CRC Committee's view on this line of argument.

[20] *Travaux Préparatoires* (UN Doc. E/CN.4/1989/48, 1989), para. 439; reproduced in S. Detrick (ed.), *A Guide to the 'Travaux préparatoires'* (Dordrecht/Boston/London, Martinus Nijhoff Publishers, 1992), pp. 368–369.

of the CRC (the right to an adequate standard of living).[21] Moreover, in its concluding observations, it has lumped together social security and standard of living, and sometimes also social security (and standard of living) with childcare services and facilities,[22] under the more general heading of basic health and welfare.[23] In the reporting guidelines, the right to benefit from social security is dealt with under the cluster heading of 'basic health and welfare'.[24] Articles 26 and 27 are indeed closely related.[25] However, Article 26 of the CRC, if read in light of other human rights and ILO treaties, could be given a more technical reading, thus imposing more specific obligations on the State than Article 27 does.

The CRC Committee has mainly paid attention to the right to benefit from social security in an instrumental way, *i.e.* to the extent that it is beneficial for the realisation of the general principles or other rights in the CRC, such as the right to survival and development[26] and the right to health,[27] or for the reduction of poverty.[28] The CRC Committee has attributed a high rate of abandonment of children and of abortion,[29] an increase in the number of young homeless people, the high rate of divorce and the number of single-

---

[21] See, *e.g.*, CRC Committee, *Concluding Observations: Gabon* (UN Doc. CRC/C/15/Add.171, 2002), para. 52(c).

[22] See, *e.g.*, CRC Committee, *Concluding Observations: Nepal* (UN Doc. CRC/C/15/Add.261, 2005), para. 72; *Nigeria* (UN Doc. CRC/C/15/Add.257, 2005), para. 59; *Antigua and Barbuda* (UN Doc. CRC/C/15/Add.247, 2004), para. 55; *Georgia* (UN Doc. CRC/C/15/Add.222, 2003), para. 53.

[23] See, *e.g.*, CRC Committee, *Concluding Observations: Latvia* (UN Doc. CRC/C/LVA/CO/2, 2006).

[24] CRC Committee, *General Guidelines Regarding the Form and Content of Initial Reports to be Submitted by States Parties Under Article 44, paragraph 1(a), of the Convention* (UN Doc. CRC/C/5, 1991), para. 19; CRC Committee, *General Guidelines Regarding the Form and Content of Periodic Reports to be Submitted by States Parties Under Article 44, paragraph 1(b) of the Convention* (UN Doc. CRC/C/58/Rev.1, 2005), VI.

[25] S. Detrick, *A Commentary on the United Nations Convention on the Rights of the Child* (The Hague, Kluwer Law International, 1999), p. 446.

[26] CRC Committee, *General Comment No. 7: Implementing Child Rights in Early Childhood* (UN Doc. CRC/C/GC/7, 2005), para. 10.

[27] CRC Committee, *General Comment No. 3: HIV/AIDS and the Rights of the Child* (UN Doc. CRC/C/GC/3, 2003), para. 6.

[28] CRC Committee, *General Comment No. 7: Implementing Child Rights in Early Childhood* (UN Doc. CRC/C/GC/7, 2005), para. 26: 'Implementing children's right to benefit from social security, including social insurance, is an important element of any strategy aimed at reducing poverty in early childhood.' Compare CRC Committee, *Concluding Observations: Trinidad and Tobago* (UN Doc. CRC/C/TTO/CO/2, 2006), paras. 57–58; *Nepal* (UN Doc. CRC/C/15/Add.261, 2005), paras. 72 and 74; *Nigeria* (UN Doc. CRC/C/15/Add.257, 2005), paras. 59 and 60 (b); *Antigua and Barbuda* (UN Doc. CRC/C/15/Add.247, 2004), paras. 55 and 56; *Georgia* (UN Doc. CRC/C/15/Add.121, 2000), paras. 50–51.

[29] CRC Committee, *Concluding Observations: Ukraine* (UN Doc. CRC/C/15/Add.42, 1995), para. 26.

parent families and teenage pregnancies,[30] or the weakening of the family structure[31] *inter alia* to the inadequacy of the social security system of a given State. More generally, it can be argued that the right to benefit from social security is particularly relevant for those who have been identified as vulnerable groups of children, such as street children, children with disabilities, displaced children, refugee and asylum-seeking children, and children belonging to racial, ethnic, religious, linguistic or other minorities. For these vulnerable groups of children in particular, social security schemes, and in particular children's benefits, could either prevent them from becoming vulnerable, or make them less vulnerable by providing a minimum material base. It is therefore surprising that the CRC Committee has hardly paid any attention *e.g.* to the right to benefit from social security in its recent general comment on the rights of children with disabilities.[32]

Clear linkages could also be established between the right to benefit from social security and the right to be protected from economic exploitation (Article 32 of the CRC). Social security benefits which ensure child maintenance, such as children's allowances, may be instrumental in making the economic activity of children unnecessary.[33] This may in turn contribute to the realisation of the right to education.

18. In indicating the instrumental value of the right to social security for the disencouragement of harmful traditional practices, the CRC Committee

---

[30] CRC Committee, *Concluding Observations: United Kingdom* (UN Doc. CRC/C/15/Add.34, 1995), para. 15. See also CRC Committee, *Concluding Observations: Belarus* (UN Doc. CRC/C/15/Add.17, 1994), para. 15.

[31] CRC Committee, *Concluding Observations: Cape Verde* (UN Doc. CRC/C/15/Add.168, 2001), para. 37.

[32] CRC Committee, *General Comment No. 9: The Rights of Children with Disabilities* (UN Doc. CRC/C/GC/9/2006). In paragraph 20, mention is made in passing of the need to ensure that resources allocated to children with disabilities are sufficient for *inter alia* social security. Para. 14 refers to care and assistance free of charge, where possible. The CRC Committee has occasionally paid attention to the right to social security of children with disabilities, *e.g.* by urging States to extend payment benefits to all children with disabilities, including those between 16 and 18 years of age (CRC Committee, *Concluding Observations: Georgia* (UN Doc. CRC/C/15/Add.222, 2003), para. 53).
The CESCR Committee has specified that adequate income support is to be provided to persons with disabilities. That support should reflect the special needs for assistance and other expenses associated with disability. The Committee has also added that institutionalisation of persons with disabilities cannot be regarded as an adequate substitute for the social security (and income-support) rights of these persons (CESCR Committee, *Draft General Comment No. 20, The Right to Social Security (Article 9)* (UN Doc. E/C.12/GC/20/CRP.1, 2006), para. 21).

[33] See G. Van Bueren, *The International Law on the Rights of the Child* (Dordrecht/Boston/London, Martinus Nijhoff Publishers, 1995), p. 268.

has not so much focused on the right *of children* to benefit from social security, but rather on the right of adults to social security. The CRC Committee has recommended taking remedial measures in the field of social security with regard to the rights of adults, so as to avoid families' over-dependence on their children, in particular providing them with care in their old age.[34] This over-dependence on children for care in the old age is thought to 'have contributed to the perpetuation of harmful traditional practices and attitudes such as a preference for boys, to the detriment of the protection and promotion of the rights of girls and of disabled children.'[35]

19. The CESCR Committee considers the right to social security, as guaranteed in Article 9 of the CESCR, as instrumental in realizing the rights to family protection, an adequate standard of living[36] and access to health care (Articles 10, 11 and 12 of the CESCR).[37] Nonetheless, it has also recognized the importance of the right in itself, and devoted attention to it without reference to its instrumental value. The CRC could take a similar approach, as the recognition of the right to benefit from social security in its more technical aspects may offer more specific guarantees in certain circumstances.

---

[34] CRC Committee, *Concluding Observations: China* (UN Doc. CRC/C/15/Add.56, 1996), para. 32.
[35] *Ibid.*, para. 12.
[36] See, *e.g.*, CESCR Committee, *Concluding Observations: Uzbekistan* (UN Doc. E/C.12/UZB/CO/1, 2006), para. 22.
[37] CESCR Committee, *Draft General Comment No. 20, The Right to Social Security (Article 9)* (UN Doc. E/C.12/GC/20/CRP.1, 2006), paras. 1, 2, 9, 11(a)(ii), 12.

CHAPTER THREE

SCOPE OF ARTICLE 26

20. The CRC Committee has so far not comprehensively clarified its understanding of Article 26 of the CRC, *e.g.* by way of a general comment. Nor has systematic attention been paid to the right to benefit from social security in the concluding observations on reports of States Parties. Guidance for a better and more comprehensive understanding of this right is therefore to be sought in the jurisprudence of other supervisory bodies, primarily the CESCR Committee and the ECSR. A second reason for paying attention to the jurisprudence of the CESCR Committee and the ECSR is that the right of a child is to *benefit from* social security, and not necessarily a direct right or claim *to* social security. Often, it will be adults rather than children who have a direct claim to social security benefits, including children's benefits, and who are therefore also the first beneficiaries of benefits.

1. *The Right 'to Benefit from'*

21. Contrary to social security provisions in other human rights treaties, Article 26 of the CRC does not guarantee the right to social security, but the right *to benefit from* social security. The reason behind this formulation is that in general, the right to receive social security benefits is granted to the parent or the guardian, not to the child itself, for the former are responsible for the maintenance of the child.[38]

However, the logic of Article 26(1) of the CRC does not seem to have been carried on into the second paragraph. The wording of Article 26(2), in which reference is made to 'application for benefits made *by* or on behalf of the child' (emphasis added), makes clear that the CRC does not exclude that a child itself is entitled to social security benefits, and is even the applicant. In its reporting guidelines for periodic reports, the CRC Committee asks States to 'indicate [. . .] the circumstances under which children themselves

---

[38] *Travaux Préparatoires* (UN Doc. E/CN.4/1984/71, 1984), para. 81; reproduced in S. Detrick (ed.), *o.c.* (note 20), pp. 364–365.

are allowed to apply for social security measures, either directly or through a representative.'[39] In its concluding observations on the report of Saint Lucia, the Committee expressed concern that 'legal provisions ensuring the right of the child to [. . .] seek social security, as well as the criteria with which benefits are granted, [had] not been developed in Saint Lucia' and recommended that the State 'review its legislation pertaining to the child's right to social security, paying specific attention to the child's right to request social security grants and benefits [. . .]'.[40] The fact that the Netherlands deemed it necessary to make a reservation to the effect that the 'provisions [of Article 26] shall not imply an independent entitlement of children to social security, including social insurance', seems to confirm the CRC Committee's interpretation.

2. 'Social Security'

22. A distinction is often being made, in particular in the context of the (R)ESC,[41] between social security, social assistance, and social welfare or social protection. Social welfare or social protection are the more general and comprehensive notions, which cover both social security and social assistance.[42] The distinction between social security and social assistance tends to be based on the purpose and the conditions attached to a benefit. Benefits for which 'individual *need* is the main criterion for eligibility, without any requirement of affiliation to a social security scheme aimed to cover a particular risk, or any requirement of professional activity or payment of contributions', are considered as social assistance (emphasis added). Social assistance benefits are a kind of savings net or fall-back position, in the sense that 'assistance is given when no social security benefit ensures that the person concerned has sufficient resources or the means to meet the cost of treatment necessary' in a person's state of health, for example.[43]

---

[39] CRC Committee, *General Guidelines Regarding the Form and Content of Periodic Reports to be Submitted by States Parties Under Article 44, paragraph 1(b) of the Convention* (UN Doc. CRC/C/58/Rev.1, 2005), para. 100.

[40] CRC Committee, *Concluding Observations: Saint Lucia* (UN Doc. CRC/C/15/Add.258, 2005), paras. 59 and 60.

[41] Where social security and social assistance are guaranteed in two separate provisions, *i.e.* Articles 12 and 13 of the (R)ESC.

[42] ECSR, 'General consideration on certain areas covered by the Charter: social protection, General Introduction', *Conclusions* XIII-4, pp. 35–36.

[43] *Ibid.*, p. 36. Compare L. Samuel, *o.c.* (note 9), p. 285. See also *Travaux Préparatoires* (UN Doc. E.CN.4/SR.221, p. 19 (Jenks, ILO)), where the notion 'social assistance' was said to relate to social welfare measures taken on the basis of the means test.

Social security is considered as a socially more advanced means of social protection, evolved out of social assistance.[44] Social security covers 'allowances related to certain risks (sickness, disablement, maternity, family, unemployment, old age, death, widowhood, vocational accidents and illnesses).' These allowances are 'not intended to compensate for a potential state of need which could result from the risk itself.'[45]

23. In light of the references to social welfare or protection in both Articles 26 and 27 of the CRC, and the decision of the drafters to retain nevertheless Article 26 (*Cf. supra* No. 16), it is suggested to give to the latter Article a strict and technical reading, *i.e.* as covering a number of specific risks and branches which have been elaborated upon by the ILO, as is done by the ECSR. In support of this reading, it is noteworthy that Article 27(3) refers to material *assistance* in case of *need*. Article 27(1) of the CRC can be understood as a general guarantee to an adequate standard of living, which is specified in both Articles 26 (social security) and 27(3) (social assistance) of the CRC. This reading corresponds to the CRC Committee's occasional approach in which it considered social security and social safety nets as components of social protection:

> [. . .] that the general lack of financial resources cannot be used as a justification for neglecting to establish social security programmes and social safety nets to protect the most vulnerable groups of children. Accordingly, it is the opinion of the Committee that a serious review should be undertaken to determine the consistency of the economic and social policies being developed with the State party's obligations under the Convention, in particular articles 26 and 27, especially with respect to the establishment or improvement of social security programmes and other social protection.[46]

24. Article 26 of the CRC refers to 'social security, *including social insurance*'. Usually, social security and social insurance are used more or less as corresponding terms. Lamarche specifies that social insurance is nevertheless different from social security, in that 'social insurance refers to a technique of providing social security benefits to workers and their families at the national level.'[47] The reason for inclusion probably lies in consistency with the CESCR.[48] Article 9 of the CESCR too explicitly refers to social insurance

---

[44] ECSR, *Conclusions* VII: France.
[45] ECSR, 'General consideration on certain areas covered by the Charter: social protection, General Introduction', *Conclusions* XIII-4, p. 36.
[46] CRC Committee, *Concluding Observations: Nigeria* (UN Doc. CRC/C/15/Add.61, 1996), para. 33.
[47] L. Lamarche, *l.c.* (note 4), p. 90.
[48] *Travaux Préparatoires* (UN Doc. E/CN.4/1989/48, 1989), para. 439; reproduced in S. Detrick (ed.), *o.c.* (note 20), pp. 368–369.

as an element of social security. The reference to social insurance in the CRC was included following a suggestion in that sense after UNICEF and the Secretariat had reviewed the draft text.[49]

This begs the question why social insurance was included in the CESCR. At the time of drafting, a debate took place on the precise meaning of social security, and whether or not it included social insurance. Social security was said to be understood in the broad sense, *i.e.* 'embracing not only individual social security, but also family allowances and the other means of social protection covered by Article 23(3) of the Universal Declaration of Human Rights.'[50] Social insurance was understood to mean individual social security of the worker.[51] In the CESCR Committee's interpretation, the reference to social insurance relates to contribution-based schemes, 'which typically involve compulsory contributions from beneficiaries, employers (where relevant), and sometimes the State, and payment of benefits and administrative expenses from a common fund.'[52]

25. Conceptually, the notion of social security thus covers both contributory and not-contributory benefits, *i.e.* benefits which are conditional respectively unconditional on the prior payment of contributions. The CRC Committee does not really distinguish between contributory and non-contributory social security schemes and/or benefits. Quite rightly so, for the distinction seems to have lost almost any practical meaning. A grand chamber of the European Court of Human Rights has held in the case of *Stec and others v. the United Kingdom* that every assertable right to a social security benefit falls under the protection of the right to property, regardless of the fact whether that benefit is contributory or not:

> If, however, a Contracting State has in force legislation providing for the payment as of right of a welfare benefit – whether conditional or not on the prior payment of contributions – that legislation must be regarded as generating a proprietary interest falling within the ambit of Article 1 of Protocol No. 1 for persons satisfying its requirements.[53]

---

[49] *Ibid.*, para. 436; reproduced in S. Detrick (ed.), *o.c.* (note 20), p. 368.
[50] *Travaux Préparatoires* (UN Doc. E/CN.4/SR.220 (Cassin, France)), p. 12.
[51] *Travaux Préparatoires* (UN Doc. A/2929), p. 211.
[52] CESCR Committee, *Draft General Comment No. 20, The Right to Social Security (Article 9)* (UN Doc. E/C.12/GC/20/CRP.1, 2006), para. 3.
[53] ECtHR (GC, rec), Nos 65731/01 and 65900/01, *Stec and others v. the United Kingdom*, 6 July 2005, paras. 47–53.

Similarly, in the ECSR's definition of social security allowances, no distinction is made between contributory, non-contributory or combined allowances. The Committee has recognized that there is a clear tendency within the Council of Europe towards the creation of benefits unconnected with contributions.[54]

3. State Obligations under Article 26 of the CRC

3.1. Reporting Obligations

26. The CRC Committee's reporting guidelines are not very specific on the information to be provided in relation to Article 26. States are to report on the right to benefit from social security under the cluster heading of basic health and welfare, in which one sub-section is devoted to 'social security and child care services and facilities' (Articles 26 and 18(3) of the CRC). In their *initial* report, States are to provide relevant information, including the principal legislative, judicial, administrative or other measures in force; the institutional infrastructure for implementing policy in this area, particularly monitoring strategies and mechanisms; and factors and difficulties encountered and progress achieved in implementing the relevant provisions of the Convention.[55] In *periodic* reports, relevant information is to be given as to follow-up, comprehensive national programmes, monitoring, allocation of budgetary and other resources, statistical data and factors and difficulties.[56]

More in particular with regard to the right to benefit from social security, issues to be addressed include: 'measures adopted to recognize for every child the right to benefit from social security, including social insurance; necessary measures taken to achieve the full realization of this right in accordance with the national law; and the manner in which the benefits

---

[54] However, in the context of the (R)ESC, the distinction is not devoid of all meaning. Only in the case of contributory benefits, no residence requirement is permitted for nationals of other States Parties to the (R)ESC. The appendix to Article 12(4) of the (R)ESC explicitly provides for the possibility of a residence requirement for non-contributory social security benefits (*Cf. infra* No. 41).

[55] CRC Committee, *General Guidelines Regarding the Form and Content of Initial Reports to be Submitted by States Parties Under Article 44, paragraph 1(a), of the Convention* (UN Doc. CRC/C/5, 1991), para. 19.

[56] CRC Committee, *General Guidelines Regarding the Form and Content of Periodic Reports to be Submitted by States Parties Under Article 44, paragraph 1(b) of the Convention* (UN Doc. CRC/C/58/Rev.1, 2005), para. 30 *juncto* para. 6.

granted take into account the resources and the circumstances of the child and of the persons having responsibility for his or her maintenance, as well as any other considerations relevant to an application for benefits made by or on behalf of the child.'[57] Reports are also to indicate 'the legal provisions relevant to the implementation of this right, the circumstances under which children themselves are allowed to apply for social security measures, either directly or through a representative, the criteria taken into account to grant the benefits, as well as any relevant disaggregated information concerning the coverage and financial implications of such measures, its incidence by age, gender, number of children per family, civil status of the parents, the situation of single parents, and the relationship of social security to unemployment.'[58]

27. The CESCR Committee's reporting guidelines offer more detailed guidance to a State's reporting obligations under the right to social security. The CRC Committee should consider adopting them *mutatis mutandis*,[59] for they correspond more to a technical reading of the right to benefit from social security, as was earlier proposed. The following information is requested for inclusion in initial reports submitted under the CESCR. States are in the first place to indicate which of the nine traditional branches of social security exist (medical care, cash sickness benefits, maternity benefits, old-age benefits, invalidity benefits, survivors' benefits, employment injury benefits, unemployment benefits and family benefits). For each existing branch, the main features of the schemes in force are to be described, indicating the comprehensiveness of the coverage provided, both in the aggregate and with respect to different groups within the society, the nature and level of benefits, and the method of financing the schemes. States are to indicate what percentage of their GNP as well as of their national and/or regional budget(s) is spent on social security, and how that compares with the situation 10 years ago. When formal (public) social security schemes are supplemented by informal (private) arrangements, these arrangements and the inter-relationships between them and the formal (public) schemes are to be described.

---

[57] CRC Committee, *General Guidelines Regarding the Form and Content of Periodic Reports to be Submitted by States Parties Under Article 44, paragraph 1(b) of the Convention* (UN Doc. CRC/C/58, 1996), para. 99.

[58] *Ibid.*, para. 100.

[59] Taking for example into account that not all branches may be directly applicable to children.

Furthermore, States are asked to indicate whether there are any groups which do not enjoy the right to social security at all or which do so to a significantly lesser degree than the majority of the population. Particular attention is paid to the situation of women in that respect. States are to indicate what measures are regarded as necessary in order to realize the right to social security for the groups mentioned; to explain the policy measures they have taken, to the maximum of their available resources, to implement the right to social security for these groups (including a calendar and time-related benchmarks for measuring their achievements in this regard); and to describe the effect of these measures on the situation of the vulnerable and disadvantaged groups in point, and report the successes, problems and shortcomings of such measures.

In the event of subsequent reports, States are to give a short review of changes, if any, in national legislation, court decisions, as well as administrative rules, procedures and practices during the reporting period affecting the right to social security. Finally, the role of international assistance in the full realisation of the right to social security is to be described.[60]

3.2. Substantive Obligations

28. The CESCR Committee usually defines a right by using the interrelated elements of availability, accessibility (including non-discrimination) and quality. The CRC Committee has occasionally adopted this approach as well.[61] There is a general obligation under both the CRC and the CESCR for progressive realisation of the economic, social and cultural rights enumerated in the respective treaties (Article 4 of the CRC; Article 2(1) of the CESCR). Article 12 of the (R)ESC offers comparable guarantees: the existence or maintenance of a system of social security; a minimum standard; the progressive improvement of the system; and non-discrimination.

The following general substantive obligations for States under the right to benefit from social security can therefore be identified: the establishment of a system of social security (availability); the progressive improvement of

---

[60] CESCR Committee, *Revised General Guidelines Regarding the Form and Contents of Reports to be Submitted by States Parties under Articles 16 and 17 of the International Covenant on Economic, Social and Cultural Rights* (UN Doc. E/C.12/1991/1, 1991).

[61] See CRC Committee, *General Comment No. 4, Adolescent Health and Development in the Context of the Convention on the Rights of the Child* (UN Doc. CRC/GC/2003/4, 2003), para. 41.

that system; accessibility (including non-discrimination) and quality. The quality of a social security system is to be explored in light of *inter alia* its personal scope, the level of benefits and the range of benefits/risks covered. As to the latter, the CRC Committee has predominantly paid attention to health care and family benefits.

Availability: the Establishment of a System of Social Security
29. A first component of the right to benefit from social security is the availability or existence of a system of social security. The CRC Committee has paid only scant attention to the obligation for States to establish or maintain a system of social security in the first place. Occasionally, it has expressed concern at the absence of a comprehensive legislative and regulatory social security system that was in full compliance with Article 26 of the Convention.[62] It has recommended to provide adequate financial resources to the social security system,[63] and emphasized

> that the general lack of financial resources cannot be used as a justification for neglecting to establish social security programmes and social safety nets to protect the most vulnerable groups of children. Accordingly, it is the opinion of the Committee that a serious review should be undertaken to determine the consistency of the economic and social policies being developed with the State party's obligations under the Convention, in particular articles 26 and 27, especially with respect to the establishment or improvement of social security programmes and other social protection.'[64]

30. Other supervisory bodies in the field of economic, social and cultural rights have put more emphasis on the need for the existence of a system of social security. Their approaches could serve as a source of inspiration for the CRC Committee. The CESCR Committee has made clear that the right to social security 'implies that a *system*, whether composed of a single or variety of schemes, is available and in place [...]. The system should be established under national law, and public authorities must take responsibility for the effective administration or supervision of the system.'[65]

---

[62] CRC Committee, *Concluding Observations: Nepal* (UN Doc. CRC/C/15/Add.261, 2005), para. 72; *Nigeria* (UN Doc. CRC/C/15/Add.257, 2005), para. 59; *Antigua and Barbuda* (UN Doc. CRC/C/15/Add.247, 2004), para. 55.
[63] CRC Committee, *Concluding Observations: Nepal* (UN Doc. CRC/C/15/Add.261, 2005), para. 73 (d).
[64] CRC Committee, *Concluding Observations: Nigeria* (UN Doc. CRC/C/15/Add.61, 1996), para. 33.
[65] CESCR Committee, *Draft General Comment No. 20, The Right to Social Security (Article 9)* (UN Doc. E/C.12/GC/20/CRP.1, 2006), para. 11(a)(i).

Moreover, to 'ensure access to the minimum essential level of social security that is essential for acquiring water and sanitation, foodstuffs, essential primary health care and basic shelter and housing, and the most basic forms of education', has been qualified as a core obligation for States.[66] Core obligations are of immediate effect. However, the CESCR Committee has weakened the meaning of core obligations in the context of the right to social security by adding that resource constraints are to be taken into account.[67] It would nevertheless be difficult to attribute the complete absence of a system of social security to the lack of available resources, for there is a general obligation to take steps, which applies immediately.[68] Also, the CESCR Committee has encouraged States to add new risks to the system,[69] and has qualified the absence of certain benefits as running counter to the obligation to progressively realize the right to social security[70] or in violation of a substantive provision.[71]

In the view of the European Committee of Social Rights, fulfilment of the obligation under Article 12(1) of the (R)ESC to establish or maintain a system of social security does not require all branches of social security to be covered. Nevertheless, certain major risks should be covered, as well as a significant percentage of the population. Moreover, effective benefits in several areas are to be offered.[72] The following branches have been identified as major risks: health care, sickness, unemployment, old age, employment injury, family,[73] and maternity.[74] At least some of them, like health

---

[66] *Ibid.*, para. 49(a). Other core obligations include: non-discrimination, the adoption and implementation of a national social security strategy and plan of action; monitoring and the adoption of social assistance programmes that protect disadvantaged and marginalized individuals and groups (*Ibid.*, para. 49(b–e)).

[67] *Ibid.*, para. 50.

[68] *Ibid.*, para. 30.

[69] *E.g.* unemployment (CESCR Committee, *Concluding Observations: China - Hong Kong* (UN Doc. E/C.12/1/Add.107, 2005), para. 94), or work accidents and occupational diseases (CESCR Committee, *Concluding Observations: Kuwait* (UN Doc. E/C.12/1/Add.98, 2004), paras. 19 and 39; CESCR Committee, *Concluding Observations: Saint Vincent and the Grenadines* (UN Doc. E/C.12/1/Add.21, 1997), para. 19).

[70] *I.e.* unemployment benefits, see CESCR Committee, *Concluding Observations: Syria* (UN Doc. E/C.12/1/Add.63, 2001), paras. 22 and 39.

[71] The absence of maternity benefits was considered to be in violation of Article 10 of the CESCR, see CESCR Committee, *Concluding Observations: Switzerland* (UN Doc. E/C.12/1/Add.30, 1998), para. 15. Compare CESCR Committee, *Concluding Observations: Saint Vincent and the Grenadines* (UN Doc. E/C.12/1/Add.21, 1997), para. 21.

[72] ECSR, 'General consideration on certain areas covered by the Charter: social protection, General Introduction', *Conclusions XIII–4*, p. 37.

[73] For family benefits see also ECSR, *Conclusions XVII–1* (vol. 2): *Turkey*.

[74] Not in conformity: Turkey, see ECSR, *Conclusions XVIII–1*.

care, sickness, family and maternity, are also highly relevant from a CRC perspective. Furthermore, it is important that a significant percentage of the population is covered. In a case in which the conditions for payment of family allowances were so stringent that they resulted in a manifestly insufficient number of persons being protected, the family benefits branch of social security was judged to be rendered inexistent.[75] A similar assessment has so far not been made by the CRC Committee.

A social security system in conformity with Article 12(1) of the (R)ESC must also be offering adequate benefits (*Cf. infra* No. 45), and be collectively funded, *i.e.* not only by contributions from employees but also from employers, and by the state budget.[76]

31. The CRC Committee has so far not given any indication of a minimum standard applicable to the social security system. In line with the view of the CESCR Committee, it could hold that a social security system is minimally to provide for the coverage of income security, access to health care and family support, in sofar as they relate to children.[77]

Progressive Realisation
32. Article 26 of the CRC on the right to benefit from social security cannot be read in isolation of the general obligation contained in Article 4 of the CRC. In the latter provision, States undertake to take all appropriate measures for the implementation of the economic, social and cultural rights recognized in the CRC 'to the maximum extent of their available resources and, where needed, within the framework of international co-operation.' In the view of the CRC Committee, '[t]he second sentence of article 4 reflects a realistic acceptance that lack of resources – financial and other resources – can hamper the full implementation of economic, social and cultural rights in some States; this introduces the concept of "progressive realization" of such rights [. . .].'[78]

During the negotiations on Article 26 of the CRC, the nature of the States Parties' obligations was the subject of some amendment proposals. Both

---

[75] ECSR, *Conclusions* XV–2Add: *Slovak Republic*.
[76] See *e.g.*, ECSR, *Conclusions* XVIII–1: *Netherlands*.
[77] These issues relate to the rights to family protection, an adequate standard of living and access to health care in the subsequent Articles 10–12 of the CESCR. Parallel provisions can be found in the Articles 18(2), 24 and 27 of the CRC.
[78] CRC Committee, *General Comment No. 5, General Measures of Implementation of the Convention on the Rights of the Child (Arts. 4, 42 and 44, para. 6)* (UN Doc. CRC/GC/5, 2003), para. 7.

Canada and the United States suggested language that was not mandatory and that implied that the right to benefit from social security was a *goal* the realisation of which would be a matter of progressive realisation. The words 'to ensure' were therefore replaced by 'to recognize'.[79] Clearly, no obligation of immediate implementation was intended by the drafters, but rather one of progressive realisation. This was stressed by the initial insertion in para. 2 of a reference to the 'national resources available'.[80] In the end, the reference in para. 2 to national resources was deleted, with the express understanding that Article 4 on the availability of resources applied to Article 26 as well.[81]

The CRC Committee has so far not really expressed itself on the requirement of progressive realisation of the right to benefit from social security. The concerns expressed with regard to Malta's reservation to Article 26,[82] *i.e.* that it was only bound 'by the obligations arising out of this article to the extent of present social security legislation', may nevertheless indicate some embryonic concern with it.[83] It has also criticized the Nigerian government for lack of *improvement* of social security programmes.[84] It is submitted that the CRC Committee should insist more on the need of progressive realisation of the right to benefit from social security, in line with Article 4 of the CRC. The jurisprudence of the CESCR Committee, which the CRC Committee has explicitly endorsed,[85] and of the ECSR (albeit to a lesser extent), may offer useful guidance.

33. Progressive realisation is the hallmark of the CESCR. The CESCR Committee has developed a doctrine on progressive realisation, which it has also applied to the right to social security. In Article 2(1) of the CESCR, a State Party undertakes to 'take steps' 'to the maximum of its available resources, with a view to achieving progressively the full realization of the rights recognized' in the CESCR. This provision reflects the acknowledgement of constraints for

---

[79] *Travaux Préparatoires* (UN Doc. E/CN.4/1984/71), paras. 83 and 87; reproduced in S. Detrick (ed.), *o.c.* (note 20), pp. 365–366.

[80] *Ibid.*, paras. 83 and 87; reproduced in S. Detrick (ed.), *o.c.* (note 20), p. 366.

[81] *Travaux Préparatoires* (UN Doc. E/CN.4/1989/48), paras. 449–450; reproduced in S. Detrick (ed.), *o.c.* (note 20), p. 370.

[82] CRC Committee, *Concluding Observations: Malta* (UN Doc. CRC/C/15/Add.129, 2000), para. 6.

[83] Malta has meanwhile withdrawn its reservation.

[84] CRC Committee, *Concluding Observations: Nigeria* (UN Doc. CRC/C/15/Add.61, 1996), para. 33.

[85] CRC Committee, *General Comment No. 5, General Measures of Implementation of the Convention on the Rights of the Child (Arts. 4, 42 and 44, para. 6)* (UN Doc. CRC/GC/5, 2003), paras. 5 and 8.

the immediate full realisation of economic, social and cultural rights, due to the limits to available resources. However, a number of obligations are considered to be of immediate effect. One such immediate obligation is to guarantee that the right is exercised without discrimination.[86] Another is the obligation to take steps, which are deliberate, concrete and targeted towards full realisation. In order to progressively reach the goal of universal coverage, States are to take steps so that coverage is significantly increased over time.[87] When recommending to ensure that the basic component of pensions was to be raised to the minimum subsistence level, the Committee acknowledged that the realisation thereof would take time, owing to limited resources, and therefore insisted on giving priority to raising the *minimum* pension levels and to ensuring that social benefits were *targeted* to the families most in need.[88] More generally, when striving for universal coverage, priority is to be given to the disadvantaged and marginalized groups in society.[89] This prioritisation in particular has been strongly emphasized in the concluding observations of the CRC Committee too (*Cf. infra* No. 36).

The logical flipside of an obligation for progressive realisation is that retrogressive measures are in principle not acceptable. There is therefore 'a strong presumption that retrogressive measures taken in relation to the right to social security are prohibited under the Covenant.' A State that deliberately takes retrogressive measures has 'the burden of proving that they have been introduced after the most careful consideration of all alternatives and that they are duly justified by reference to the totality of the rights provided for in the Covenant in the context of the full use of the State party's maximum available resources.' Retrogressive measures in the field of social security will therefore have to pass a six-fold test under the CESCR: 1. whether alternatives have been comprehensively examined; 2. whether there has been genuine participation of affected groups in examining proposed measures and alternatives; 3. whether the measures are discriminatory; 4. whether the measures will have a sustained impact on the realization of the right to social security; 5. whether the individual has been

---

[86] CESCR Committee, *Draft General Comment No. 20, The Right to Social Security (Article 9)* (UN Doc. E/C.12/GC/20/CRP.1, 2006), para. 30.

[87] CESCR Committee, *Concluding Observations: Colombia* (UN Doc. E/C.12/1/Add.74, 2001), para. 39.

[88] CESCR Committee, *Concluding Observations: Russian Federation* (UN Doc. E/C.12/1/Add.94, 2003), para. 50.

[89] CESCR Committee, *Concluding Observations: Jamaica* (UN Doc. E/C.12/1/Add.75, 2001), para. 23; CESCR Committee, *Concluding Observations: Korea* (UN Doc. E/C.12/1995/3, 1995), para. 22.

deprived of access to the minimum essential level of social security unless all maximum available resources have been used, including domestic and international; and 6. whether review procedures at the national level have examined the reforms.[90] In practice, the CESCR Committee has mainly expressed concern about the needs of disadvantaged and vulnerable groups in society, such as young families with children.[91] While not qualifying it as retrogressive measures, it recommended Canada to revise its policy and to re-establish a programme which included universal entitlements, national standards and a legally enforceable right to adequate assistance.[92] Given the CRC Committee's statement that the CESCR Committee's general comment on Article 2(1) of the CESCR 'should be seen as complementary' to its own on general measures of implementation,[93] the assumption of the prohibition of retrogressive measures can be assumed to be integrated in the CRC Committee's jurisprudence too.

34. The (R)ESC does not contain a *general* clause on progressive realisation and availability of resources. Nevertheless, the ECSR has adopted in its case law the following rule:

> When the achievement of one of the rights in question is exceptionally complex and particularly expensive to resolve, a State Party must take measures that allows it to achieve the objectives of the Charter within a reasonable time, with measurable progress and to an extent consistent with the maximum use of available resources. States Parties must be particularly mindful of the impact that their choices will have for groups with heightened vulnerabilities as well as for others persons affected including, especially, their families on whom falls the heaviest burden in the event of institutional shortcomings.[94]

Article 12 of the (R)ESC on the right to social security contains, in its paragraph 3, an explicit reference to progressive realisation. States undertake 'to endeavour to raise progressively the system of social security to a higher level.' This 'dynamic' provision requires States to 'make a continuous effort

---

[90] CESCR Committee, *Draft General Comment No. 20, The Right to Social Security (Article 9)* (UN Doc. E/C.12/GC/20/CRP.1, 2006), para. 31.

[91] See, *e.g.*, CESCR Committee, *Concluding Observations: Germany* (UN Doc. E/C.12/1/Add.68, 2001), paras. 23 and 41; CESCR Committee, *Concluding Observations: the Netherlands* (UN Doc. E/C.12/1/Add.25, 1998), paras. 16 and 25; *Finland* (UN Doc. E/C.12/1/Add.8, 1996), para. 21.

[92] CESCR Committee, *Concluding Observations: Canada* (UN Doc. E/C.12/1/Add.31, 1998), paras. 20–40.

[93] CRC Committee, *General Comment No. 5, General Measures of Implementation of the Convention on the Rights of the Child (Arts. 4, 42 and 44, para. 6)* (UN Doc. CRC/GC/5, 2003), para. 5.

[94] ECSR, No. 13/2, *International Association Autism-Europe v. France*, 4 November 2003, para. 53.

to bring their social security systems progressively to a higher level'.[95] It should therefore be possible 'to observe improvements on the previous situation, reflecting a gradual raising of the social security system of the country in question above the level required by International Labour Convention No. 102.'[96]

The ECSR's approach is instructive in the way the assessment of progress can be done pragmatically, so that requirements of progressive realisation and non-retrogressive measures do not impose unrealistic obligations on States Parties, in particular those Parties who face serious economic recession. For the ECSR, the assessment of progress is first of all a general one: the question is whether, *overall*, there has been more progress than regression. *E.g.*, in the field of health care, the ECSR has held that an increase in cost-sharing by beneficiaries for medical consultations, but whereby the disadvantaged population groups' ability to pay is taken into account, and whereby there is a significant decrease in the average level of patients' contributions, is in conformity with the Charter.[97] A similar assessment has been made in the field of unemployment[98] or family benefits.[99] Such a general assessment has also been favoured by the Inter-American Court of Human Rights. Article 26 of the American Convention too holds an obligation to progressively realize economic, social and cultural rights. In the case of the reduction of pensions of some individuals, the individuals concerned claimed that the reduction of their pensions was in violation of Article 26 of the American Convention. The Inter-American Court of Human Rights held however that progressive development belonged to the *collective* dimension of economic, social and cultural rights, and that no individual cases were to be assessed in light of this obligation.[100] The court thus seems to argue that progressive development is not to be assessed on an individual basis, but rather in the context of a general and overall evaluation of the pension regime.[101]

---

[95] ECSR, *Conclusions* I, pp. 62 and 200.
[96] ECSR, *Conclusions* III, p. 63. Under the Revised ESC, the reference treaty is the European Code of Social Security.
[97] ECSR, *Conclusions* XV–1, vol. 1: *Belgium*.
[98] ECSR, *Conclusions* XV–1, vol. 2: *Portugal*.
[99] ECSR, *Conclusions* XV–1, vol. 1: *France*.
[100] IACtHR, *Five pensioners v Peru*, 28 February 2003, Series C No. 98, para. 147.
[101] See H.F. Ledesma, 'The Validity of Economic, Social and Cultural Rights in the Inter-American System', in: M. Windführ (ed.), *Beyond the Nation State – Human Rights in Times of Globalization* (Uppsala, Global Publications Foundation, 2005), p. 207.

35. Secondly, when confronted with retrogressive measures, the ECSR has developed a pragmatic approach and applied the objective and reasonable justification test, rather than to choose a principled rejection of all retrogressive measures. Regarding the aim or goal pursued, retrogressive ('restrictive') measures seem only acceptable if they 'appear necessary to ensure the maintenance of a given system of social security'.[102] The Committee has given a broad meaning to safeguarding the social security system: the consolidation of public finances, in order to avoid mounting deficits and debt interest,[103] the introduction of measures to confront demographical changes, and the adoption of measures to render social protection more conducive to employment have all been deemed necessary for the maintenance of a social security system.[104] Two negative conditions have been added: retrogressive measures or restrictions should 'not prevent members of society from continuing to enjoy effective protection against social and economic risks, and there [should be] no tendency to gradually reduce the social security system to one of minimal support.'[105] The latter seems to constitute the bottom-line in light of the common feature of European social security systems, *i.e.* the 'endeavour to protect all those who may be subject to any of the dangers covered, despite the ageing of the population and even though priority is given to job creation'.[106]

However, the pursuance of a legitimate objective is not sufficient to satisfy the requirement of progressive improvement. In addition, the ECSR also examines whether the measures taken to reduce expenditure on social security are justified, *i.e.*, 'whether they are adapted to the financial situation which has brought them about.'[107] In other words, the European Committee of Social Rights will evaluate the appropriateness of the retrogressive measures taken in relation to the objective pursued, in light of the consequences of the measures, in order to determine whether they are justified.[108] The adoption of measures to offset shortcomings in the social welfare system following the adoption of restrictive legislation or policies does not influence

---

[102] ECSR, 'General consideration on certain areas covered by the Charter: social protection, General Introduction', *Conclusions* XIII–4, p. 143.
[103] ECSR, *Conclusions* XIV–1: *Austria*.
[104] ECSR, *Conclusions* XIV–1: *Finland*.
[105] ECSR, *Conclusions* XIV-1: *Netherlands*.
[106] ECSR, 'General consideration on certain areas covered by the Charter: social protection, General Introduction', *Conclusions* XIII–4, p. 42.
[107] ECSR, *Conclusions* XIV–1: *Austria*.
[108] ECSR, *Conclusions* XVI–1, vol. 2: *Poland*, p. 542.

the decision on compliance with the requirements of Article 12(3).[109] More generally, one of the criteria is whether the burden of reforms does not weigh too heavily on the economically most vulnerable households.[110]

The ECSR has applied this approach *inter alia* with regard to health insurance, which has been an area of retrogressive social security reform in many European countries. Reforms introduced by Germany were judged 'not [to have] been manifestly disproportionate to the end being pursued', primarily because it had sought to preserve 'a compulsory health insurance system based on solidarity, spreading the burden of the risks among the members of the community.'[111] The means chosen by the Netherlands to reduce the costs of the health system however were considered to be inappropriate. In the view of the ECSR

> the goal of effective social protection for all members of society, which all states that have accepted Article 12 para. 3 must pursue, presupposes that the Contracting Parties maintain social security systems based on solidarity, as this constitutes a fundamental guarantee against discriminatory treatment in this area. The collective nature of social security funding, through contributions and/or taxation, is a key factor in this guarantee, ensuring an apportionment of the cost of the risks between the members of the group. Another important factor is the participation of the persons protected in the management and supervision of the system.[112]

The risk of sickness had been linked to the company, and the public sickness insurance scheme had been made subsidiary for the majority of workers. The funding of the health insurance branch in the Netherlands was therefore no longer secured on a collective basis for the majority of workers. This situation was found not to be in conformity with Article 12(3) of the ESC.[113]

The ECSR's approach may guide the CRC Committee in assessing retrogressive measures in a judge-like manner, so as to preserve the principle of non-retrogressive measures while at the same time not to impose unrealistic obligations on States Parties, in particular those Parties who face serious economic recession.

---

[109] ECSR, 'General consideration on certain areas covered by the Charter: social protection, General Introduction', *Conclusions* XIII–4, pp. 41–42.
[110] ECSR, *Conclusions* XIV–1: *Finland*.
[111] ECSR, *Conclusions* XIV–1: *Germany*.
[112] ECSR, *Conclusions* XIV–1: *Netherlands*.
[113] *Ibid.*

Personal Coverage: Physical Accessibility

36. Article 26 of the CRC guarantees the right to benefit from social security for every child. In its concluding observations, the CRC Committee has paid attention to the (risk of) exclusion of certain marginalized groups, such as female-headed households,[114] non-working parents,[115] and parents and children most in need of such assistance.[116] It has also focused on 16- to 18-year-olds,[117] including children with disabilities between that age range,[118] children who had been granted a temporary protection visa (those arriving in the country without any travel document),[119] children of unemployed or self-employed parents,[120] and economically disadvantaged children below the age of 18 years.[121] The CRC Committee has equally paid attention to the limited social security coverage (of children) per se.[122] As the beneficiaries of the right are not necessarily children themselves (Cf. *supra* No. 21), in its scrutiny of the personal coverage offered by social security systems the CRC Committee has quite logically not restricted itself to children, but also made recommendations on social security benefits more generally, to the extent that they *related* to children.[123]

The ultimate goal of the CRC Committee is clearly universal social security coverage of all children and their families within a given State Party.[124]

---

[114] CRC Committee, *Concluding Observations: Trinidad and Tobago* (UN Doc. CRC/C/TTO/CO/2, 2006), paras. 57–58.

[115] CRC Committee, *Concluding Observations: Pakistan* (UN Doc. CRC/C/15/Add.217, 2003), para. 59 (c).

[116] CRC Committee, *Concluding Observations: Congo* (UN Doc. CRC/C/15/Add.153, 2001), para. 58.

[117] CRC Committee, *Concluding Observations: United Kingdom* (UN Doc. CRC/C/15/Add.188, 2002), para. 46 (b).

[118] CRC Committee, *Concluding Observations: Georgia* (UN Doc. CRC/C/15/Add.222, 2003), para. 53.

[119] CRC Committee, *Concluding Observations: Australia* (UN Doc. CRC/C/15/Add.268, 2005), para. 64.

[120] CRC Committee, *Concluding Observations: Mexico* (UN Doc. CRC/C/MEX/CO/3, 2006), para. 54.

[121] CRC Committee, *Concluding Observations: United Kingdom (Isle of Man)* (UN Doc. CRC/C/15/Add.134, 2000), paras. 32–33.

[122] CRC Committee, *Concluding Observations: Morocco* (UN Doc. CRC/C/15/Add.211, 2003), para. 52; *Mozambique* (UN Doc. CRC/C/15/Add.172, 2002), para. 54 (d); *Cameroon* (UN Doc. CRC/C/15/Add.164, 2001), para. 52; *Côte d'Ivoire* (UN Doc. CRC/C/15/Add.155, 2001), para. 48; *Central African Republic* (UN Doc. CRC/C/15/Add.138, 2000), para. 66.

[123] Explicitly so for example with regard to Georgia: the CRC Committee endorsed the recommendation made by the Committee on Economic, Social and Cultural Rights *as this related to children* (CRC Committee, *Concluding Observations: Georgia* (UN Doc. CRC/C/15/Add.222, 2003), para. 53).

[124] CRC Committee, *Concluding Observations: the Sudan* (UN Doc. CRC/C/15/Add.190, 2002), para. 52; *Netherlands Antilles* (UN Doc. CRC/C/15/Add.186, 2002), para. 45 (g).

States have therefore been encouraged to implement 'measures through which a significantly larger number of children and their families may benefit from a minimum of social security protection.'[125] The inclusion of persons not paying contributions to the social security system has been welcomed.[126] At a minimum, children from poorer families and communities, including rural communities, are to have access to basic health and other services which are either free or within their means.[127]

37. The CRC Committee's approach concurs with the CESCR Committee's stance that 'all persons should be *covered* by the social security system, including the most disadvantaged or marginalized sections of the population, in law and in fact.'[128] In its concluding observations, the CESCR Committee has expressed concern about the exclusion of many low-income persons from the social security system, long waiting periods or residence requirements for new applicants,[129] the limited personal scope of sickness and maternity insurance,[130] and the strict eligibility conditions for unemployment benefits.[131] It has encouraged States *inter alia* to increase the personal coverage of unemployment[132] and pension[133] benefits, to ensure universal access to affordable primary health care and to include all members of society in the compulsory health insurance scheme.[134] Central to the Committee's

---

[125] CRC Committee, *Concluding Observations: Mozambique* (UN Doc. CRC/C/15/Add.172, 2002), para. 55 (b). Compare CRC Committee, *Concluding Observations: Yemen* (UN Doc. CRC/C/15/Add.267, 2005), para. 62 (c); *Congo* (UN Doc. CRC/C/15/Add.153, 2001), para. 59.

[126] CRC Committee, *Concluding Observations: Portugal* (UN Doc. CRC/C/15/Add.162, 2001), para. 28.

[127] CRC Committee, *Concluding Observations: Central African Republic* (UN Doc. CRC/C/15/Add.138, 2000), para. 67.

[128] CESCR Committee, *Draft General Comment No. 20, The Right to Social Security (Article 9)* (UN Doc. E/C.12/GC/20/CRP.1, 2006), para. 11(a)(ii). On the obligation of universal coverage, compare CESCR Committee, *Concluding Observations: North Korea* (UN Doc. E/C.12/1/Add.95, 2003), para. 17; *Jamaica* (UN Doc. E/C.12/1/Add.75, 2001), paras. 10 and 23; *Dominican Republic* (UN Doc. E/C.12/1/Add.16, 1997), para. 38.

[129] CESCR Committee, *Concluding Observations: China – Hong Kong* (UN Doc. E/C.12/1/Add.107, 2005), para. 84; *Australia* (UN Doc. E/C.12/1/Add.50, 2000), para. 32.

[130] CESCR Committee, *Concluding Observations: Ecuador* (UN Doc. E/C.12/1/Add.100, 2004), para. 21.

[131] CESCR Committee, *Concluding Observations: Lithuania* (UN Doc. E/C.12/1/Add.96, 2004), para. 17.

[132] CESCR Committee, *Concluding Observations: Uzbekistan* (UN Doc. E/C.12/UZB/CO/1, 2006), para. 53; *Serbia and Montenegro* (UN Doc. E/C.12/1/Add.108, 2005), para. 47; *Lithuania* (UN Doc. E/C.12/1/Add.96, 2004), para. 39.

[133] CESCR Committee, *Concluding Observations: Zambia* (UN Doc. E/C.12/1/Add.106, 2005), para. 43; *Chile* (UN Doc. E/C.12/1/Add.105, 2004), para. 43.

[134] CESCR Committee, *Concluding Observations: Serbia and Montenegro* (UN Doc. E/C.12/1/Add.108, 2005), para. 60.

concerns is the need to ensure that all workers and all those in need, in particular disadvantaged and marginalized groups, are adequately covered.[135] Self-employed workers, domestic workers, rural workers, workers in the informal economy, low-income groups, non-resident workers and women are to be included.[136] In case of a private social security system, special measures are to be taken to assist groups who are not able to pay into that system.[137] Non-nationals are not to be excluded from the social security system, and should be accorded equal treatment as nationals.[138]

Child benefits targeting low-income families are not to be restricted to *working* parents only, but should be extended to all low-income families. The CESCR Committee has recommended not to give them only to *working* poor parents, but to all low-income families, also those dependent on social assistance.[139] The CRC Committee shares this concern (*Cf. supra* No. 36), although it has not yet said explicitly so with regard to child benefits in particular.

Non-Discrimination
38. One dimension of accessibility is whether a social security system is accessible for all without discrimination on any of the prohibited grounds. Non-discrimination is one of the four general principles of the CRC, and considered to be part of the core obligations that are incumbent on States Parties to the CESCR. The CRC Committee has addressed in particular instances of discrimination on the grounds of gender and nationality. It has thus for example recommended ensuring that social security benefits are extending equally for boys and girls attending full-time education beyond the age of 18 years.[140]

---

[135] CESCR Committee, *Concluding Observations: China - Hong Kong* (UN Doc. E/C.12/1/Add.107, 2005), para. 96; *Chile* (UN Doc. E/C.12/1/Add.105, 2004), para. 43; *Moldova* (UN Doc. E/C.12/1/Add.91, 2003), para. 39; *Brazil* (UN doc. E/C.12/1/Add.87, 2003), para. 50.

[136] CESCR Committee, *Concluding Observations: Ecuador* (UN Doc. E/C.12/1/Add.100, 2004), para. 44; *Guatemala* (UN Doc. E/C.12/1/Add.93, 2003), para. 35; *Yemen* (UN Doc. E/C.12/1/Add.92, 2003), paras. 13 and 32; *Benin* (UN Doc. E/C.12/1/Add.78, 2002), paras. 17 and 36; *Honduras* (UN Doc. E/C.12/1/Add.57, 2001), para. 39; *Saint Vincent and the Grenadines* (UN Doc. E/C.12/1/Add.21, 1997), para. 19; *Dominican Republic* (UN Doc. E/C.12/1/Add.16, 1997), para. 21; *Portugal - Macau* (UN Doc. E/C.12/1/Add.9, 1996), paras. 13 and 21.

[137] CESCR Committee, *Concluding Observations: Chile* (UN Doc. E/C.12/1/Add.105, 2004), para. 43; *Mexico* (UN Doc. E/C.12/1/Add.41, 1999), para. 24.

[138] CESCR Committee, *Concluding Observations: Kuwait* (UN Doc. E/C.12/1/Add.98, 2004), paras. 20 and 40.

[139] CESCR Committee, *Concluding Observations: Canada* (UN Doc. E/C.12/1/Add.31, 1998), para. 44.

[140] CRC Committee, *Concluding Observations: Cyprus* (UN Doc. CRC/C/15/Add.205, 2003), paras. 49–50.

The CESCR Committee has emphasized that special attention is to be given to 'those individuals and groups who have traditionally faced difficulties' in exercising the right to social security, among which children and dependents.[141] Particular attention is also given to orphans. They should not be excluded from social security schemes on the prohibited grounds of discrimination, and be given assistance in access to social security schemes.[142] The CRC Committee has so far not paid much attention to discrimination against orphans in the field of social security.

39. The CRC Committee has expressed concern about social security laws which effectively deprive non-citizens of rights to social security benefits,[143] and recommended that all children *residing* on the territory of a State party equally enjoy social benefits.[144] Similarly, the CESCR Committee has held that non-nationals, refugees, asylum seekers and stateless persons should be able to access non-contributory social security schemes for income and family support, as well as health care. Restrictions should be proportionate and reasonable.[145] In its concluding observations, the CESCR Committee has expressed concern about *de facto* discrimination against internal migrants in the field of social security.[146] The ECtHR has argued that very weighty reasons have to be put forward to regard a difference in treatment based exclusively on the ground of nationality[147] and sex[148] to be compatible with the ECHR. In the field of social security benefits, it has held that differential treatment solely based on nationality, between on the one hand French citizens or citizens of a state with which a reciprocal agreement had been signed, and on the other hand other foreigners, had no objective and reasonable justification and was in violation of Article 14 of the ECHR.[149]

---

[141] CESCR Committee, *Draft General Comment No. 20, The Right to Social Security (Article 9)* (UN Doc. E/C.12/GC/20/CRP.1, 2006), para. 15.

[142] *Ibid.*, paras. 24–25.

[143] CRC Committee, *Concluding Observations: Uzbekistan* (UN Doc. CRC/C/15/Add.167, 2001), para. 26; *Kyrgyzstan* (UN Doc. CRC/C/15/Add.127, 2000), para. 21.

[144] CRC Committee, *Concluding Observations: Czech Republic* (UN Doc. CRC/C/15/Add.201, 2003), para. 53.

[145] *Ibid.*, paras. 28–29.

[146] CESCR Committee, *Concluding Observations: China* (UN Doc. E/C.12/1/Add.107, 2005), paras. 15–16.

[147] EctHR, No. 40892/98, *Koua Poirrez v France*, 30 September 2003, para. 46.

[148] EctHR (GC), Nos 65731/01 and 65900/01, *Stec and others v the United Kingdom*, 12 April 2006, para. 52.

[149] *Ibid.*, paras. 46–50.

40. The European Committee of Social Rights has examined some nationality and residency issues in more detail. This jurisprudence might offer useful guidance to the CRC Committee, were it to examine discrimination in the field of social security in more detail. A first question is whether making family benefits dependent on a prescribed period of residence of the parents on the territory of the State Party amounts to indirect discrimination.[150] In principle, the imposition of nationality, length of residence or employment requirements to non-nationals for eligibility for children allowance is not in conformity with the Charter.[151] Art. 12(4) of the (R)ESC allows for one exception, however.

Art. 12(4) of the (R)ESC aims to ensure the application of the traditional principles of international social security law, *i.e.* equal treatment for nationals of other States Parties, and coordination. It applies to all traditional branches of social security, including *e.g.* medical care, and sickness and family benefits.[152] This equality principle means that States Parties are not allowed to grant entitlement to social security benefits solely to their own nationals or to nationals of specific States Parties,[153] nor to impose additional conditions on nationals of other States Parties.[154] To the latter rule, one exception applies, based on the Appendix to Article 12(4) of the (R)ESC: with regard to non-contributory benefits (such as child benefits) for nationals of other States Parties, a condition of completion of a prescribed period of residence is allowed. However, the Committee reserves the right to assess the proportionality of the imposed length of residence.[155] It has thus found

---

[150] The Committee has addressed this issue both under Article 12(4) and 16 of the (R)ESC. In order to adopt the same stance for the family benefits that are treated under both provisions, the Committee has considered that a length of residence condition is permitted in application of Article 16 under the same conditions as in application of Article 12(4) (see ECSR, General Introduction, *Conclusions* XIV–1, para. 71 and *e.g.*, ECSR, *Conclusions* XV–2, add.: *Slovak Republic*).

[151] ECSR, *Conclusions* XVII–1, vol. 1: *Austria*.

[152] ECSR, *Conclusions* XIII–4, p. 42.

[153] The nationality requirement attached to the entitlement to the supplement child-raising allowance in certain Länder in Germany was found to be discriminatory (ECSR, *Conclusions* XVI–1, vol. 1: *Germany*); ECSR, *Conclusions* XIII–4, pp. 404–405). Under Article 16: child benefit only to children with Slovenian nationality: direct discrimination: ECSR, *Conclusions* 2002: *Slovenia*.

[154] Subjecting the payment of family allowances to the condition that the person concerned had been in employment for more than three months, was considered to constitute discrimination (ECSR, *Conclusions* XVII–1, vol. 1: *Austria*).

[155] ECSR, 'General consideration on certain areas covered by the Charter: social protection, General Introduction', *Conclusions* XIII–4, pp. 43–44. On the contrary, a length of residence requirement of one year for receipt of unemployment benefits, which are contributory benefits, is not in conformity with the Charter (ECSR, *Conclusions* XVIII–1: *Czech Republic*).

five[156] and three years[157] to be excessive. Six months or one year residence requirements have been deemed to be reasonable and manifestly not excessive.[158]

41. Subjecting the payment of family benefits to a residence requirement in respect of the *children* potentially affects non-nationals more than nationals, and therefore represented yet another case of indirect discrimination in the view of the ECSR.[159] While to non-contributory benefits like child benefits, the exception of the Appendix to Article 12(4) of the (R)ESC at first sight seems applicable, the ECSR found it was not, for the application of a condition of residence was only allowed with respect to *beneficiaries, i.e.* the children's parents.[160] However, the amount of the allowance could be reduced for children not residing in the country of the beneficiary provided that the cost of living in the children's country of residence was significantly lower, and that the discrepancy in benefit was proportional to the difference in these costs.[161] The Committee reserved the right to assess the proportionality of any reduction.[162] One Committee member criticized this so-called exportability principle, for he believed that a family allowance was not to be connected anymore to the worker, but was rather meant to compensate the costs children gave rise to for their parents or guardians:

> The recipient is no longer the working parent as was often the case in the past, but the factual carer of the child. Instead of being conceived as an income supplement for the worker, the child allowance/family benefit has become a universal means of support for children or child families.[163]

---

[156] ECSR, *Conclusions* XV–1: *Belgium*.

[157] ECSR, *Conclusions* XVI–1, vol. 2: *Poland*: the qualifying period of at least three years period was considered not to be of a reasonable duration, in the context of the fact that since Poland had not accepted Article 13(1), families from other Contracting Parties lawfully residing in Poland were not entitled under the Charter to receive social assistance.

[158] ECSR, *Conclusions* XV–2, add.: *Slovak Republic*; ECSR, *Conclusions* XV–1, vol. 2: *Sweden*.

[159] ECSR, *Conclusions* 2004–2: *Lithuania*; ECSR, *Conclusions* XVII–2, vol. 2: *Latvia*; ECSR, *Conclusions* XV–1: *Belgium*. Compare many other countries as of 14th reporting cycle (see L. Samuel, *o.c.* (note 9), pp. 300–301).

The Committee reconfirmed its position under the Revised European Social Charter (ECSR, General Introduction, *Conclusions* 2004, vol. 1, pp. 9 and 10, para. 6).

[160] ECSR, *Conclusions* XIII–4, p. 44.

[161] ECSR, *Conclusions* XV–1, vol. 1: *France*.

[162] ECSR, *Conclusions* XIII–4, pp. 44–45.

[163] See, *e.g.*, ECSR, *Conclusions* 2004–2: *Lithuania*, Article 12(4), Dissenting Opinion of Mr. M. Mikkola.

In 2006, the Committee reversed its position, without further explanation, and deemed a residence requirement in respect of children henceforth in conformity with Article 12(4) of the (R)ESC.[164]

Another issue the CRC Committee might be confronted with is the existence of a difference between children of own nationals and children of nationals of other Parties, in age limit under which children are regarded as dependent. For the ECSR, this differentiation amounts to discrimination if no objective justification can be invoked.[165] Such a justification was found to be absent in the different upper age limit for eligibility for dependence benefit in France, which was as high as twenty in respect of the children of French nationals (where the child concerned is studying, engaged on an apprenticeship or in vocational training), while it was limited to fifteen years for Turkish nationals residing in France, but whose children were resident in Turkey.[166]

42. Whether persons *illegally* residing on the territory qualify for social security benefits is unclear. The CRC Committee's recommendation that all children *residing* on the territory of a State party equally enjoy social benefits seems to suggest they do.[167] The CESCR Committee has kept silent on this, except for the claim that emergency medical care should not be refused by reason of a person's nationality or residency status.[168] In the context of the (R)ESC, much depends on the bilateral and multilateral agreements concluded in accordance with Article 12(4) of the (R)ESC. Moreover, the Appendix to the RESC limits the personal scope of the RESC to include only foreigners in so far as they are nationals of other States Parties and lawfully resident or working regularly within the territory of a given State Party. The ECSR has held that with regard to the right to medical care for children, which is 'a right of fundamental importance to the individual since it is connected to the right to life itself and goes to the very dignity of the human being',[169] 'legislation or practice which denies entitlement to medical assistance to foreign nationals, within the territory of a State Party, even if they

---

[164] ESCR, *Conclusions 2006: General Introduction*, para. 22.

[165] ECSR, *Conclusions XV–1, vol. 1: France*.

[166] *Ibid.*

[167] CRC Committee, *Concluding Observations: Czech Republic* (UN Doc. CRC/C/15/Add.201, 2003), para. 53.

[168] CESCR Committee, *Draft General Comment No. 20, The Right to Social Security (Article 9)* (UN Doc. E/C.12/GC/20/CRP.1, 2006), para. 40.

[169] ECSR, No. 14/2003, *International Federation of Human Rights Leagues (FIDH) v France*, 4 November 2003, para. 30.

are there illegally, is contrary to the Charter.'[170] However, the Committee believes that the restriction of the Appendix impacts differently on each right as guaranteed in the Articles 1–17. It is therefore uncertain whether the ECSR would adopt the same reasoning with regard to the right to social security.

43. The CRC Committee has encouraged States Parties to strengthen the provision of information on social security benefits to children and families 'from some distinct ethnic, religious, linguistic or cultural groups, such as the Roma', for they were 'not fully aware of their rights to social security and welfare and [were] consequently unable to claim such assistance.'[171] It is thus ahead of the ECSR, which has started only recently to ask questions as to whether Roma families are equally treated in law and in practice with respect to family benefits.[172] Going beyond the narrow principle of equal treatment for nationals of other States Parties, a broader notion of non-discrimination is required, *i.e.* not limited to the *nationality* ground, nor to nationals of other States *Parties* to the (R)ESC.[173]

44. Yet another issue of discrimination with respect to social security benefits has been raised with the Human Rights Committee, which has addressed differential treatment of children born out of wedlock. In *Derksen v. The Netherlands*, the Committee held that a distinction between children born either in wedlock or after a given date also out of wedlock on the one hand, and children born out of wedlock prior to that date on the other hand, was not based on reasonable grounds and constituted (indirect) discrimination. In the view of the Committee, the termination of ongoing discrimination in respect of children who have no say in whether their parents choose to marry or not, should have taken place by extending the application of the new law, which was aimed at remedying the situation, to children born out of wedlock prior to a certain date, albeit not necessarily with retroactive effect.[174]

---

[170] *Ibid.*, para. 32.

[171] CRC Committee, *Concluding Observations: Greece* (UN Doc. CRC/C/15/Add.170, 2002), paras. 62–63.

[172] Article E of the RESC explicitly prohibits discrimination on a number of prohibited grounds. It is not an autonomous right: 'its function is to help secure the equal effective enjoyment of all the rights concerned regardless of difference.' (ECSR, *Conclusions 2004-2: Slovenia*).

[173] ECSR, No. 13/2002, *International Association Autism Europe* v *France*, 4 November 2003, para. 51.

[174] Human Rights Committee, No. 976/2001, *Derksen* v *The Netherlands* (UN Doc. CCPR/C/80/D/976/2001), para. 9.3. For a more elaborate discussion of this and other cases of non-

Quality

Adequacy of Benefits

45. The CRC Committee has repeatedly expressed concern about the low level of social security benefits[175] and the non- or delayed payment of *inter alia* child allowances.[175] It has recommended measures to improve and make transparent the payments of allowances to families with children.[177] What the CRC Committee considers to be adequate is not always clear: sometimes it has referred to a vague threshold of 'a minimum of social security for the child and the family'.[178] Specifically with regard to family allowances, the criterion applied is whether every child enjoys the right to an adequate standard of living.[179]

The CESCR Committee has equally established a strong link between the right to social security and the right to an adequate standard of living in order to assess the adequacy of benefits. In the view of the CESCR Committee, benefits must be adequate in amount and duration. The yardstick to measure adequacy is primarily the realisation of the rights to family protection, an adequate standard of living[180] and access to health care, complemented by the principle of human dignity and the right to non-discrimination.[181] In application of these principles, States have been encouraged to increase the minimum pension amounts in order to strengthen the role of pensions as a safety net,[182] and to put in place a system of indexing the level of basic

---

discrimination as dealt with by the Human Rights Committee, see *inter alia* W. Vandenhole, *Non-Discrimination and Equality in the View of the UN Human Rights Treaty Bodies* (Antwerp/Oxford, Intersentia, 2005), pp. 112–135.

[175] CRC Committee, *Concluding Observations: Georgia* (UN Doc. CRC/C/15/Add.222, 2003), para. 54; *Moldova* (UN Doc. CRC/C/15/Add.192, 2002), para. 39.

[176] CRC Committee, *Concluding Observations: Russian Federation* (UN Doc. CRC/C/15/Add.110, 1999), para. 13.

[177] CRC Committee, *Concluding Observations: Moldova* (UN Doc. CRC/C/15/Add.192, 2002), para. 40(b).

[178] CRC Committee, *Concluding Observations: Solomon Islands* (UN Doc. CRC/C/15/Add.208, 2003), para. 45(b); *Czech Republic* (UN Doc. CRC/C/15/Add.201, 2003), para. 43(b).

[179] CRC Committee, *Concluding Observations: Hungary* (UN Doc. CRC/C/HUN/CO/2, 2006), para. 46.

[180] Compare CESCR Committee, *Concluding Observations: Uzbekistan* (UN Doc. E/C.12/UZB/CO/1, 2006), para. 22; *China – Hong Kong* (UN Doc. E/C.12/1/Add.107, 2005), para. 84; *Italy* (UN Doc. E/C.12/1/Add.103, 2004), para. 52; *Denmark* (UN Doc. E/C.12/1/Add.102, 2004), para. 27; *Estonia* (UN Doc. E/C.12/1/Add.85, 2002), para. 17.

[181] CESCR Committee, *Draft General Comment No. 20, The Right to Social Security (Article 9)* (UN Doc. E/C.12/GC/20/CRP.1, 2006), para. 11(a)(ii). See also CESCR Committee, *Concluding Observations: United Kingdom – Hong Kong* (UN Doc. E/C.12/1994/19, 1994), para. 40.

[182] CESCR Committee, *Concluding Observations: Uzbekistan* (UN Doc. E/C.12/UZB/CO/1, 2006), para. 53.

pensions reflecting changes in the cost of living.[183] No trade-off is permis-
sible between universal coverage and adequacy: adequacy should not come
at the detriment of the number of beneficiaries covered.[184] The lowest level
of unemployment benefit is to be sufficient to secure a decent standard of
living for a worker and his/her family.[185] More generally, social security
benefits are to come close(r) to the subsistence minimum.[186]

A more stringent approach has been taken by the ECSR. For the ECSR,
income-replacement benefits levels should stand in reasonable proportion
to the previous income, and they should never fall below the poverty threshold.[187]Since 2004, the ECSR has systematically made reference to the poverty
threshold (defined as 50 per cent of median equivalized household income,
as calculated on the basis of the Eurostat at-risk-of-poverty threshold value)
when assessing benefit levels.[188] The CRC Committee might consider to apply
a formal (regionally or nationally defined) threshold too when assessing the
adequacy of social security benefits as they relate to children.

Aggregation of a benefit which is under the poverty threshold with means-
tested kinds of benefits should not be accepted as bringing the situation
into conformity with the right to social security.[189]

Risks Covered
46. The CRC Committee has singled out two risks in particular in its concluding observations, *i.e.* firstly, health care and health insurance, and secondly, family allowances. It can be assumed that these are most directly
relevant to children, although other risks should not be excluded *a priori.*

---

[183] CESCR Committee, *Concluding Observations: Lithuania* (UN Doc. E/C.12/1/Add.96, 2004),
para. 38.
[184] CESCR Committee, *Concluding Observations: Azerbaijan* (UN Doc. E/C.12/1/Add.104, 2004),
para. 43.
[185] CESCR Committee, *Concluding Observations: Estonia* (UN Doc. E/C.12/1/Add.85, 2002),
para. 40.
[186] CESCR Committee, *Concluding Observations: Georgia* (UN Doc. E/C.12/1/Add.83, 2002),
para. 35.
[187] See, *e.g.,* ECSR, *Conclusions* XVIII–1: *Netherlands.*
[188] Governmental Committee of the European Social Charter, *Report Concerning Conclusions
2004,* Strasbourg, 8 April 2005, T-SG (2004)26, para. 210.
The ECSR has so far twice reached the conclusion that a situation was not in conformity
with Article 12(1) for inadequacy of benefits: with regard to the level of benefits for the
elderly and unemployment benefits in respect of Lithuania (ECSR, *Conclusions* 2004: Lithuania),
and to the level of the unemployment benefit for a single person in respect of Austria (ECSR,
Conclusions XVIII–1: Austria).
[189] See, *e.g.,* ECSR, *Conclusions* XVIII–1: *United Kingdom.*

Health Care and Health Insurance

47. The CRC Committee has insisted on the creation of a social security system for better health access for children.[190] With regard to the cost of health insurance, it has recommended to lower the cost of health services,[191] or to restore free access to health services for children.[192] It has also asked to ensure that psychological treatments for children are covered by the national social security system.[193]

With regard to adolescent health, the CRC Committee has insisted on providing particular support to pregnant teenagers, including through community structures and social security benefits,[194] and on reviewing policies for young mothers under the age of 16 years with regard to allowance entitlements and parenting courses.[195]

Child Allowances or Benefits

48. Not surprisingly, the CRC Committee has mainly paid attention in its concluding observations to child allowances or benefits. The primary focus has been on vulnerable families and families living in poverty. The CRC Committee believes that a social security policy and child benefits can play an important role in furthering the rights of children, supporting responsible parenthood and assisting vulnerable and poor families.[196] The criterion in light of which a family allowance system is to be assessed seems to be whether every child enjoys the right to an adequate standard of living.[197] Following a decrease in net income of families with children caused by both

---

[190] CRC Committee, *Concluding Observations: Malawi* (UN Doc. CRC/C/15/Add.174, 2002), para. 54(d).

[191] CRC Committee, *Concluding Observations: Switzerland* (UN Doc. CRC/C/15/Add.182, 2002), para. 45.

[192] CRC Committee, *Concluding Observations: Gabon* (UN Doc. CRC/C/15/Add.171, 2002), para. 52(c).

[193] CRC Committee, *Concluding Observations: Andorra* (UN Doc. CRC/C/15/Add.176, 2002), para. 42(d).

[194] CRC Committee, *Concluding Observations: Mauritius* (UN Doc. CRC/C/MUS/CO/2, 2006), para. 55(d); *Trinidad and Tobago* (UN Doc. CRC/C/TTO/CO/2, 2006), para. 54(d); *Antigua and Barbuda* (UN Doc. CRC/C/15/Add.247, 2004), para. 54(d).

[195] CRC Committee, *Concluding Observations: United Kingdom* (UN Doc. CRC/C/15/Add.188, 2002), para. 44(b).

[196] CRC Committee, *Concluding Observations: Nicaragua* (UN Doc. CRC/C/15/Add.265, 2005), para. 37(a); *Jamaica* (UN Doc. CRC/C/15/Add.210, 2003), paras. 46–47.

[197] CRC Committee, *Concluding Observations: Hungary* (UN Doc. CRC/C/HUN/CO/2, 2006), para. 46. For the CESCR Committee, family benefits need to cover food, clothing and housing, where appropriate (see CESCR Committee, *Draft General Comment No. 20, The Right to Social Security (Article 9)* (UN Doc. E/C.12/GC/20/CRP.1, 2006), para. 26).

high unemployment rates and budgetary measures that negatively affected child-related allowances, the allocation of more funds to families with children has been strongly recommended, also in light of the favourable economic circumstances.[198] Due account is to be taken of the means-testing system, especially for families without gainful employment and self-employed families.[199]

Assistance to families *inter alia* through child benefits and family-related benefits has been welcomed,[200] in particular in the fight against poverty.[201] With regard to vulnerable families such as single-parent households, the CRC Committee has recommended to provide particular support, including through social security benefits, among others.[202]

49. A similar preoccupation with more vulnerable types of families such as single-parent families can be found in the (R)ESC. Article 16 of the (R)ESC requires States *inter alia* to guarantee an adequate standard of living (economic protection) for families, by appropriate means. To this end they must operate a family or child benefit scheme,[203] in addition to other forms of economic protection such as birth grants, additional payments to large families or tax relief.[204] A family or child benefit provided as part of social security, available either universally or subject to a means-test, should be 'the primary means' of economic protection of the family in the view of the ECSR.[205] The insistence on family and child benefits is to be seen in light of the Committee's experience that 'fiscal reform [. . .] rather [benefits] middle- and high-income families than low-income families.' In the view of the ECSR, a family policy which is mainly based on fiscal benefits has perverse effects, for non-taxable low-income households cannot receive fiscal benefits.[206]

---

[198] CRC Committee, *Concluding Observations: Finland* (UN Doc. CRC/C/15/Add.132, 2000), paras. 33–34.

[199] CRC Committee, *Concluding Observations: Switzerland* (UN Doc. CRC/C/15/Add.182, 2002), para. 47.

[200] CRC Committee, *Concluding Observations: Canada* (UN Doc. CRC/C/15/Add.215, 2003), para. 38.

[201] CRC Committee, *Concluding Observations: Austria* (UN Doc. CRC/C/15/Add.251, 2005), para. 45.

[202] CRC Committee, *Concluding Observations: Trinidad and Tobago* (UN Doc. CRC/C/TTO/CO/2, 2006), para. 42; *Nepal* (UN Doc. CRC/C/15/Add.261, 2005), para. 50; *Antigua and Barbuda* (UN Doc. CRC/C/15/Add.247, 2004), para. 38(a).

[203] ECSR, *Conclusions* XV–1, vol. 2: *Spain*.

[204] ECSR, *Conclusions* XVII–1, vol. 2: *Netherlands-Aruba*.

[205] *Ibid.*

[206] ECSR, *Conclusions* XVII–2, vol. 2: *Spain*.

Family or child benefits must constitute a sufficient income supplement to a significant number of families;[207] this requirement pertains to adequacy and availability. With regard to the availability of family benefits, the ECSR has found that a situation is not in conformity with Article 16 of the (R)ESC if there are only a limited number of beneficiaries. Such was the case in Turkey, where only a small proportion of families which belonged to privileged categories of workers (*i.e.* civil servants and employees covered by collective agreements) received family benefits,[208] and in Lithuania. In the latter country, a child benefit was only paid up to the age of 3. A means-tested benefit was paid up to age of 16 only for families raising three children. As a consequence, most families were not receiving any family benefits after the age of 3.[209]

As to the adequacy of family benefits, the ECSR has held that they are to 'represent a relevant contribution to the family income'[210] at least for low-income level families.[211] For the child allowance to be an adequate income supplement, it is to represent a significant percentage of the monthly mean equivalized net income.[212] This is a more precise, and therefore more preferable, yardstick than the CRC Committee's reference to an adequate standard of living. What a 'significant percentage' exactly amounts to, seems to depend on the scope of coverage of families and on the extent to which the child allowance or benefit is complemented by other forms of family benefits, such as tax relief and income-related benefits. While 2,9 per cent has been found to be clearly inadequate,[213] 5 per cent may be adequate, 'taking into consideration that Child Benefit is universal and that it is complemented by other forms of family benefits, mainly tax relief and benefits in kind, which are income-related'.[214] The level of benefits is to be adjusted as necessary to keep pace with inflation.[215]

---

[207] ECSR, *Conclusions* XV–1, vol. 2: *Norway*; ECSR, *Conclusions* XVI–1, vol. 2: *Poland*.

[208] ECSR, *Conclusions* XV–1, vol. 2: *Turkey*; ECSR, *Conclusions* XIII–3: *Turkey*.

[209] ECSR, *Conclusions* 2004–II: *Lithuania*.

[210] ECSR, *Conclusions* XVII–1, vol. 1: *Greece*.

[211] ECSR, *Conclusions* XVII–1, vol. 2: *Portugal*.

[212] ECSR, *Conclusions* 2004–II: *Lithuania*.

[213] ECSR, *Conclusions* XVII–2, vol. 2: *Spain*. Compare 3,37 per cent in ESC, *Conclusions* XVII–2, vol. 2: *Latvia*.

[214] ECSR, *Conclusions* XVII–1, vol. 2: *United Kingdom*. Compare also 6,3 per cent in ECSR, *Conclusions* 2004-1: *France*; 7,1 per cent in ECSR, *Conclusions* XVII–1, vol. 1: *Denmark*; 8,5 per cent in ECSR, *Conclusions* XVII–1, vol. 1: *Austria*.

[215] ECSR, *Conclusions* XVII–1, vol. 2: *Netherlands-Aruba*; ECSR, *Conclusions* XIV–1: *Germany*.

A Qualifier

50. A specific feature of the provision on social security in the CRC is the reference made to the financial circumstances of the child and his or her parents or guardians.[216] Notwithstanding initial disagreement among the negotiators on the need for such a clause, it was eventually adopted without much substantive discussion in the 1984 Working Group.[217] In 1989, the text was revised on mainly technical grounds, following suggestions by UNICEF and the Secretariat. However, a number of States, supported by the ILO, also expressed the view that the reference to circumstances and resources was redundant.[218] In light of the Working Group's inability to reach a consensus, a drafting group was established to try and find one. In the end, the references to 'the resources and the circumstances of the child and persons having responsibility for the maintenance of the child' and to 'other consideration relevant to an application for benefits made by or on behalf of the child' were kept in the text.

None of the parallel provisions in other human rights treaties contain such a clause. Making social security contingent on the caregiver's lack of resources 'reflects the fact that children's economic security is generally bound up with that of their adult caregivers'.[219] While the inclusion of a reference to the resources of adults probably had a restrictive intention, its effect may rather be to reinforce the CRC Committee's attention for social security rights of adults as they relate to children (*Cf. supra* No. 36).

---

[216] Article 26(2) of the CRC.
[217] *Travaux Préparatoires* (UN Doc. E/CN.4/1984/71, 1984), paras. 88–93; reproduced in S. Detrick (ed.), *o.c.* (note 20), pp. 366–367.
[218] *Travaux Préparatoires* (UN Doc. E/CN.4/1989/48, 1989), paras. 444–447; reproduced in S. Detrick (ed.), *o.c.* (note 20), pp. 369–370.
[219] R. Hodgkin and P. Newell, *Implementation Handbook for the Convention on the Rights of the Child* (New York, UNICEF, 2002), p. 379.

BIBLIOGRAPHY

Detrick, S. (ed.)	*A Guide to the 'Travaux préparatoires'*, Dordrecht-Boston-London: Martinus Nijhoff Publishers, 1992.
Detrick, S.	*A Commentary on the United Nations Convention on the Rights of the Child*, The Hague: Kluwer Law International, 1999.
Harris, D. and Darcy, J.	*The European Social Charter*, New York: Transnational Publishers, 2001.
Hodgkin, R. and Newell, P.	*Implementation Handbook for the Convention on the Rights of the Child*, New York: UNICEF, 2002.
Lamarche, L.	'The Right to Social Security in the International Covenant on Economic, Social and Cultural Rights', in: A. Chapman and S. Russell (eds.), *Core Obligations: Building a Framework for Economic, Social and Cultural Rights*, Antwerp-Oxford-New York: Intersentia, 2002.
Ledesma, H.F.	'The Validity of Economic, Social and Cultural Rights in the Inter-American System', in: M. Windführ (ed.) *Beyond the Nation State – Human Rights in Times of Globalization*, Uppsala: Global Publications Foundation, 2005.
Samuel, L.	*Fundamental Social Rights. Case Law of the European Social Charter*, Strasbourg: Council of Europe Publishing, 2002.
Scheinin, M.	'The Right to Social Security', in: A. Eide, C. Krause and A. Rosas (eds.), *Economic, Social and Cultural Rights*, Dordrecht-Boston-London: Martinus Nijhoff Publishers, 2001.
Van Bueren, G.	*The International Law on the Rights of the Child*, Dordrecht-Boston-London: Martinus Nijhoff Publishers, 1995.
Vandenhole, W.	*Non-Discrimination and Equality in the View of the UN Human Rights Treaty Bodies*, Antwerp-Oxford: Intersentia, 2005.
Vandenhole, W.	'Human Rights in a Globalizing Economy: Is the Right to Social Protection Qualified by a Duty to Work?', in: S. Parmentier and H. Werdmölder (eds.), *Fundamental Rights and Fundamental Responsibilities*, Antwerp-Oxford: Intersentia, 2007, forthcoming.